WISDOM LITERATURE
AND PSALMS

INTERPRETING BIBLICAL TEXTS

The Gospels, Fred B. Craddock
New Testament Apocalyptic, Paul S. Minear
The Pentateuch, Lloyd R. Bailey, Sr.
The Prophets, James M. Ward
Wisdom Literature and Psalms, Roland E. Murphy, O. Carm.

INTERPRETING **ibt** BIBLICAL TEXTS

Wisdom Literature & Psalms

Roland E. Murphy,
O.Carm.

LLOYD R. BAILEY, SR.
and
VICTOR P. FURNISH, EDITORS

ABINGDON PRESS   NASHVILLE

WISDOM LITERATURE AND PSALMS

Copyright © 1983 by Abingdon Press

Library of Congress Cataloging in Publication Data

MURPHY, ROLAND EDMUND, 1917–
    Wisdom literature and Psalms.
    (Interpreting biblical texts)
    Bibliography: p.
    1. Wisdom literature—Criticism, interpretation, etc.
    2. Bible. O.T. Psalms—Criticism, interpretation, etc.
    I. Bailey, Lloyd R., 1936-   . II. Furnish, Victor Paul.
    III. Title. IV. Series.
    BS1455.M86   1983   223'.06   82-16276

ISBN 0-687-45759-9

Scripture quotations unless otherwise noted are from the Revised Standard Version of the Bible, copyrighted 1946, 1952, 1971, © 1973, by the Division of Christian Education of the National Council of the Churches of Christ in the U.S.A., and used by permission.

Those noted NAB are from The New American Bible, copyright © 1970 by the Confraternity of Christian Doctrine, Washington, D.C.

MANUFACTURED BY THE PARTHENON PRESS AT
NASHVILLE, TENNESSEE, UNITED STATES OF AMERICA

Dedicated to my former students in both Catholic and Protestant theological schools

INTERPRETING BIBLICAL TEXTS:
Editors' Foreword

The volumes in this series have been planned for those who are convinced that the Bible has a meaning for our life today, and who wish to enhance their skills as interpreters of the biblical texts. Such interpreters must necessarily engage themselves in two closely related tasks: (1) determining as much as possible the original meaning of the various biblical writings, and (2) determining in what respect these texts are still meaningful today. The objective of the present series is to keep both of these tasks carefully in view, and to provide assistance in relating the one to the other.

Because of this overall objective it would be wrong to regard the individual volumes in this series as commentaries, as homiletical expositions of selected texts, or as abstract discussions of "the hermeneutical problem." Rather, they have been written in order to identify and illustrate what is involved in relating the meaning of the biblical texts in their own times and places to their meaning in ours. Biblical commentaries and other technical reference works sometimes focus exclusively on the first, paying little or no attention to the second. On the other hand, many attempts to expound the contemporary "relevance" of biblical themes or passages pay scant attention to the intentions of the texts themselves. And although one of the standard topics of "hermeneutics" is how a text's original meaning relates to its present meaning, such discussions often employ highly technical philosophical language and proceed with little reference to concrete examples. By way of contrast, the present volumes are written in language that will be understood by scholars, clergy, and laypersons alike, and they deal with concrete texts, actual problems of interpretation, and practical procedures for moving from "then" to "now."

Each contributor to this series is committed to three basic tasks: (1) a description of the salient features of the particular type of biblical literature or section of the canon assigned to him; (2) the identification and explanation of the basic assumptions which guide his analysis and explication of those materials; and (3) the discussion of possible contemporary meanings of representative texts, in view of the specified assumptions with which the interpreter approaches them. Considerations which should be borne in mind by the interpreter in reflecting upon contemporary meanings of these texts are introduced by the sign ● and are accentuated with a different style of type.

The assumptions which are brought to biblical interpretation may vary from one author to the next, and will undoubtedly vary from those of many readers. Nonetheless, we believe that the present series, by illustrating how careful interpreters carry out their tasks, will encourage readers to be more reflective about the way they interpret the Bible.

Lloyd R. Bailey, Sr.
Duke Divinity School

Victor P. Furnish
Perkins School of Theology
Southern Methodist University

CONTENTS

PREFACE   11

I. SCHOLARLY PRESUPPOSITIONS FOR
    UNDERSTANDING ISRAEL'S WISDOM   13
        1. The Wisdom Books 13
        2. Origins 17
        3. Ancient Near Eastern Background 21
        4. Characteristics of Wisdom Literature 25

II. INTERPRETATION   43
        1. The Presuppositions of a Modern Reader 46
        2. Lessons from the History of Exegesis 51

III. SELECTIONS FROM WISDOM LITERATURE   63
        1. Proverbs 64
        2. Job 76
        3. Ecclesiastes 85
        4. The Song of Songs (Canticles) 93
        5. Ecclesiasticus (Sirach) 100
        6. Wisdom of Solomon 106

IV. ISRAEL'S PRAYER—THE PSALMS   110
    1. Presuppositions 110
    2. Selections from Psalms 116

EPILOGUE   151

AIDS FOR THE INTERPRETER   155

PREFACE

This volume has the following goals: (1) a discussion of the presuppositions or assumptions involved in approaching the OT Wisdom Literature and the Psalms. These assumptions, it will be seen, can be classified as scholarly and/or personal. (2) An exemplification of the historical critical approach to certain selected biblical passages. (3) An indication of how the biblical text has been and can be appropriated by a later (post-biblical) generation. It is impossible to present here a sketch of the history of exegesis, but even one example from the past helps us understand where we are in the present. The history of exegesis demonstrates that readers of the Bible have gone beyond the literal historical sense in their interpretation, and the modern reader also inevitably does this in applying the Bible to his or her life. Not all the interpretations of the past command assent, but many illumine the text and teach us something about the presuppositions that we bring to our reading of the Bible.

In order to concretize biblical interpretation several selections from the Wisdom Literature and the Psalms will be analyzed from the perspective of both the historical critical meaning and the present meaning which a twentieth-century reader may find in the text.

I. SCHOLARLY PRESUPPOSITIONS FOR UNDERSTANDING ISRAEL'S WISDOM

It is not the intent of this section simply to reproduce the data that can be found in any introduction to biblical literature. Rather, we wish to point out the scholarly insights acquired over centuries which can and should be brought to bear in reading the text. For example, what conclusions about OT wisdom have gained general acceptance among scholars and serve us as an introduction to coming to grips with the text? There is basic information about the structure of Proverbs that is different from that of the Book of Job; neither book is read in the same way. Moreover, a general survey of the Wisdom Literature can provide a profitable vantage point for the understanding of an individual book. While these insights are always subject to modification and even to further increase, they are exceedingly helpful. If they are stated explicitly, we become aware of the assumptions involved in approaching this literature.

1. The Wisdom Books

By common consent "Wisdom Literature" refers to Proverbs, Job, and Ecclesiastes in the Hebrew Bible and to Ecclesiasticus (Sirach) and the Wisdom of Solomon among the Apocrypha (which Roman Catholics regard as canonical). Whatever be the differences in the "authority" of these books, all would grant that Sirach and Wisdom of Solomon are Wisdom Literature and part of the wisdom movement within the biblical period.

The phrase itself, "Wisdom Literature," has been regarded by some as a misnomer, especially as applied to similar works in ancient Egyptian and Mesopotamian literature. However, it is a convenient designation for these five books, which have in common, besides the use of the term "wisdom" (in Hebrew, ḥokmāh), certain characteristics which we shall explore.

It is important to arrive at an approximate dating of these books against the background of Israel's history. Despite the merely probable nature of the arguments that can be alleged for dating, the following schema can be proposed as a working hypothesis adopted by the majority of scholars.

Proverbs. Essentially an assembly of collections of sayings that derive largely from the preexilic period. The introduction, Proverbs 1–9, has been usually taken as a postexilic writing (fifth century?) although not all would agree. Thus, the book probably assumed its final form after the Exile.

Structure: 1–9—introduction, made up of wisdom poems and instructions

10:1–22:16—first "Solomonic" collection of sayings

22:17–24:22—sayings of the wise

24:23-34—other sayings of the wise

25–29—second "Solomonic" collection

30:1-9—words of Agur, followed by numerical sayings

31:1-9—words of Lemuel's mother

31:10-31—acrostic poem

Job. The final form of this book is probably postexilic, although some scholars contend for the exilic period or earlier. Because of the mention of Job in Ezek 14:14, 20 (along with Noah and Daniel) it is reasonable to suppose that the story of the saintly Job and how he was delivered from his trials (chaps. 1–2; 42:7-17) is quite old. That story forms the framework of the book (prologue, epilogue), into which a poetic dialogue has been inserted.

Structure: 1–2—prologue
3–31—Job's dialogue with the friends
32–37—speeches of Elihu
38:1–42:6—speeches of Yahweh and Job's response
42:7-17—epilogue

Song of Songs. This little book is included here despite the fact that it is not technically Wisdom Literature. It is a collection of love poems—exchanges of fidelity, admiration, and yearning between a man and a woman. Because the poems reflect values which were cherished in Wisdom Literature, many scholars are of the opinion that they were preserved and transmitted by Israel's sages. The superscription attributes the book to Solomon, but this is not likely. It is usually dated after the Exile, but without conclusive evidence. There is no consensus on the number of the poems contained in the eight chapters. This inconvenience is offset by the fact that most of the time one can identify who is speaking. Modern translations, such as the NAB or NEB, aid the reader by adding such indications in the margin.

Ecclesiastes. This work (also called Qoheleth) is dated by the majority of modern scholars to about 300 ±. In 1:12–2:12 the author presents himself as king over Jerusalem (Solomon, the wise one); hence the superscription describes him as "son of David, king in Jerusalem" (1:1).

Structure: No compelling analysis of the structure has yet been offered. However there is reason to think that editor(s) were responsible for the epilogue in 12:9-14 and probably for the introduction in 1:1-11. Normally throughout the work the author speaks of himself in the first person.

Ecclesiasticus. This compendium of Jewish wisdom dates from the second century B.C., probably between 200-180. The author, Ben Sira (or Sirach), wrote in Hebrew, but it was mainly the Greek translation by his grandson (and also other translations) that was used by the Western world until the last one hundred years. Then the Hebrew text came to be known, thanks to the discovery of fragments in a Jewish genizah, or storehouse, in Cairo and in the old Jewish fortress at Masada near the Dead Sea.

Structure: There is no primary structural outline of the book that can be offered here. At certain points significant hymns appear (17:1-14; 39:12-35; 42:15–43:33) and "the praise of the fathers" in 44–50 is a clearly defined unit.

Wisdom of Solomon. Written in Greek, probably in the first century B.C. in Alexandria, by a Jew of the Diaspora, writing under the name of Solomon (i.e., it is a "pseudepigraph").

Structure: 1:1–11:1—the praises of wisdom
                11:2–19:22—God's fidelity to his people at the
                time of the Exodus

The extent of Wisdom Literature has been considerably expanded in scholarly judgment in recent years. It is generally agreed that among the Apocrypha, *Baruch* 3:9–4:4 is a wisdom piece. Wisdom interests are also reflected in the *Letter of Aristeas* (to be dated probably at the end of first century B.C.)

and in the *Sayings of the Fathers* ("Avoth," as it is sometimes referred to). But even within the OT claims have been made for the wisdom character of the Joseph story (Genesis 37–50), the succession narrative (2 Samuel 9–20; 1 Kings 1–2), Deuteronomy, Esther, Amos, and certain Psalms. However, the discussion of the extent of Wisdom Literature still continues, and it is too early to say what the final scholarly verdict will be.

2. Origins

How did the Wisdom Literature come into being? Each work has its own particular history, of course, but the larger question is, What circumstances led to the beginnings of what we call Wisdom Literature? If one can point with reason to the temple worship as being the matrix of most of the Psalms, to what can one point as the origin of Wisdom Literature?

One of the insights gained by modern scholarship into the origins of almost any ancient literature is the recognition of the oral transmission of the material before it became fixed in writing. This is particularly true for OT studies where the role of oral tradition has been recognized behind the books of the Pentateuch and several of the Prophets and other works.

In the case of Israelite wisdom it is reasonable to assume that proverbial maxims and admonitions first had a life of their own within the community *before* they assumed a fixed, written form. In a world where the oral was naturally more prominent in and central to regular life, the important traditions of the family would have circulated orally and been transmitted on the basis of memory. Indeed, when one examines the proverbs and sayings, scattered in the historical books of the OT (e.g., Judg 8:21; 1 Sam 30:24-25; 2 Sam 5:8), one is able to capture the feel of oral transmission.

If the transmission of the wisdom heritage is judged to have been at first largely by word of mouth, the question still remains, Who were the originators, and who were the transmitters of the heritage? Two answers to the question have been suggested in modern scholarship: the family or tribe, and the court school where professional bureaucratic training, and especially writing, would have been cultivated. Both of these answers may be correct; there is no reason to exclude either one. The ultimate thrust of our question is, What is the life setting for this literature? And the answer, as might be expected, has to be a broad one: a teaching or didactic situation. And where is this most likely to be found? Within the ethos of a family or tribe, and also in the more formal circumstances of a "school."

How does one "prove" that these are the likely origins? There are no sources that uncover this for us. These are only inferences, but not unreasonable ones. An example of transmission of wisdom sayings and admonitions within the family is presented in the fourth chapter of the Book of Tobit. The elderly Tobit lays down recommendations to his son: "My son, when I die, bury me. . . . Seek advice from every wise man. . . . So, my son, remember my commandments, and do not let them be blotted out of your mind" (4:3, 18, 19). Moreover it is to be expected that a basic wisdom concerning life's experiences would have been transmitted from one generation to another within the tribe and within the family.

Under the impact of the discovery of Egyptian "teachings" that are similar to the Book of Proverbs, modern scholars have argued that there must have been a school for courtiers in Jerusalem similar to the school at the Egyptian court. The analogy is a reasonable one. There are several "king" sayings in Proverbs, and the "men of [King] Hezekiah" are described in Prov 25:1 as playing a role in the transmission of the work. Scholars have come to describe the Solomonic era as an age of "Enlightenment," when Israel took on the new ways of the surrounding culture, especially in the administration of the newly founded United Monarchy. Again, this is a reasonable inference. The association of wisdom with king and court is not to be disputed. However, we have no hard evidence for schools that were the centers of wisdom. And even if such institutions did cultivate the transmission of wisdom, it would not follow that they were the *source* of the wisdom movement. A more vigorous cultivation of Wisdom Literature may have taken place here, but there is no reason to leave out the role of the family or tribe in the formation of Israel's wisdom. It seems better to recognize that *both* society and school stand behind the origins and growth of Israelite wisdom.

It is worth noting in view of this discussion, that at least three of the five wisdom books are *certainly* to be dated in the postexilic period when there was no longer any king or court: Ecclesiastes, (± 300), Sirach (about 180) and the Wisdom of Solomon (first century B.C.). Qoheleth is portrayed as one who taught the people knowledge (Eccl 12:9) and Ben Sira invites his readers to "the house of instruction" (Sir 51:23, NAB). But here also in the postexilic period we have little hard evidence concerning the nature of such "schools."

Although there are unavoidable uncertainties in this survey of the channels through which Israel's wisdom heritage was transmitted, the broad outline is plausible. It is important to correlate such settings with the literature itself, as in the repeated appeal of the teacher to student in Proverbs 1–9 ("my son"). In this way one is better able to enter into the concrete reality of the sayings and instructions contained in the wisdom books. These sayings were not just floating in the air; neither were they authored or written down for the first time in the Book of Proverbs. They have a prehistory that the reader should be aware of in order to understand their purpose and frame of reference—and ultimately their meanings.

The reader may have noted that nothing thus far has been said of Solomon, to whom is attributed the Book of Proverbs; Ecclesiastes by implication (Eccl 1:1, "the son of David, king in Jerusalem"); the Wisdom of Solomon (written in Greek!); and the Song of Songs (1:1, "The Song of Songs, which is Solomon's"). How is the Solomonic "authorship" to be understood?

Biblical tradition considers Solomon as the wise man, *par excellence*. Thus he is described in 1 Kgs 4:29-30, 34: "And God gave Solomon wisdom and understanding beyond measure, and largeness of mind like the sand on the seashore, so that Solomon's wisdom surpassed the wisdom of all the people of the east, and all the wisdom of Egypt. . . . And men came . . . from all the kings of the earth, who had heard of his wisdom." Several interesting points are raised in this text. Wisdom is a gift of God, and Solomon's wisdom is compared to that of Mesopotamia and Egypt. It is almost as if Israel was aware of the international heritage of wisdom, and that she had arrived late on the wisdom scene. The text goes on to enumerate examples of "nature" wisdom ("beasts, and of birds, and of reptiles, and of fish") about which Solomon discoursed and concludes with the remark about his fame. His fame is further illustrated by the visit of the queen of Sheba (10:1-10). The nature of wisdom as gift is portrayed in the episode of his sacrifice at Gibeon (1 Kgs 3:3-14), where the Lord guarantees to give Solomon whatever he asks for. To this Solomon replies by requesting a "listening heart" *(lēb shōmēaᶜ)* "to govern thy people"—a gift that is immediately illustrated by the story of the two harlots (3:16-28, my translation).

The attribution of four books (Proverbs, Ecclesiastes, Wisdom of Solomon, the Song of Songs) to Solomon is a reflection of this strong tradition about his wisdom. But we know for certain that only part of one book (Proverbs 10–31) can be seriously considered as going back to the Solomonic era, and we have no real evidence of Solomonic authorship. The sayings in Proverbs 10–31 doubtless come from several different historical periods.

3. Ancient Near Eastern Background

It is helpful to situate Israel's Wisdom Literature against the broader background of ancient Near Eastern wisdom. We have seen above that Israel herself has done this by comparing Solomon's wisdom with that "of all the people of the east, and all the wisdom of Egypt" (1 Kgs 4:30). The wisdom of Mesopotamia and the wisdom of Egypt have become known in some detail to the Western world only in this century. Generally speaking, they provide points of similarities as well as contrasts with Israel's wisdom. Here we will limit ourselves to works that are immediately comparable to the OT books. English translations are available in the volumes of Pritchard, Lambert, Lichtheim, and Simpson, found in the "Aids for the Interpreter" at the end of this volume.

Mesopotamia. Several collections of sayings in the ancient Sumerian and Babylonian cultures have been made available in recent years. We have definite evidence of a school: the *e-dubba* ("house of tablets"), or ancient Sumerian school, where the scribes copied out the various literary works, including proverbs, as early as the third millenium B.C. Particularly noteworthy is the fact that so many of the proverbs are bilingual, both Sumerian and Akkadian. They were used for the practical purpose of learning a language, as well as for their intrinsic didactic value. From about the fourteenth/thirteenth centuries come the *Counsels of Wisdom* which are moral exhortations given by an important court figure to his "son" concerning guarded speech, avoiding disputes and disreputable companions, etc. This type of admonition is familiar to us from

the Book of Proverbs and also the Egyptian "teachings" which
we have yet to look at.

In addition to such aphoristic material, there is a reflective
type which approximates the style of the Books of Job and
Ecclesiastes. Thus, the fate of the "righteous sufferer" is
treated in a poem entitled by its first words, *Ludlul bel nemeqi*
("I will praise the lord of wisdom"). A certain nobleman relates
his sufferings and also the dreams that assure him of
deliverance. Finally, Marduk, the "lord of wisdom," saves him.
However, the literary form is that of thanksgiving for the
deliverance, and so quite different from Job or Ecclesiastes.

Another Babylonian work, *The Dialogue of Pessimism,* has
rightly been compared with Ecclesiastes, in that it deals with
concerns that he shares, and in a mood that is close to his in
spirit. It is a conversation between master and slave concerning
such subjects as women, piety, and death. To the considerations which the master advances for a given course of action the
slave replies with additional reasons. When the master then
changes his mind and argues contrary to his original proposal,
the slave agrees with him and provides more reasons. The
similarity to Ecclesiastes consists in the fact that the contra-
dictions of the human condition are shown by the dialogue.

The *Dialogue About Human Misery* (also called the
Babylonian Theodicy), which dates from about 1000 B.C., is
also comparable to Job and Ecclesiastes. It is an acrostic poem
of seven stanzas, each of eleven lines, a dialogue between a
suffering person and his friend. Whereas the "friends" in Job
are somewhat hostile, in this case the friend is clearly
sympathetic to the lament of the sufferer. Again the topics are
the problems of human existence and the ills of society: piety
and its value, the reality and even the profit of crime. There is
an admission that the gods have made humans prone to
evil—an admission that is totally foreign to the Israelite view.

What is common to all these works is the problem of the human condition, and they serve as points of comparison with the biblical writings.

The Story of Ahikar is a famous tale that has been preserved in many languages and literatures. It seems to have derived from Mesopotamia (Assyria), but the earliest form is in Aramaic, found among the fifth-century papyri discovered on the island of Elephantine in the Nile at the beginning of the twentieth century. What interests us here are the "words" that are attributed to Ahikar. They consist of sayings and fables that are in the general wisdom style. There is emphasis on training of youth (even by the rod), truthfulness, humility, and other virtues. Interestingly, wisdom is personified and spoken of in a manner that is reminiscent of Proverbs 8: "Wisdom . . . To gods also she is dear F[or all time] the kingdom is [hers]. In he[av]en is she established, for the lord of holy ones has exalted [her]."[1]

Egypt. The closest parallel to the material in the Book of Proverbs is to be found in the Egyptian *Sebayit,* "teaching," or "instruction." There are about a dozen of these, most of them associated with royal or government figures: Hor-dedef, Kagemni, Ptah-hotep, Merikare, Khety (or Duauf), Ani, Amenemhet, Amenemopet. If one adds the relatively late Insinger papyrus, these writings cover a period of about two millenia. The *Sebayit* follows a set form: "The beginning of the instruction which X made for his son (student) Y." Rules of proper conduct make up the body of the teaching, as is suggested by the introduction to the teaching of Amenemopet:

> The beginning of the teaching of life, the testimony for prosperity, all precepts for intercourse with elders, the rules for courtiers, . . . to know how to return an answer to him who said

[1]James B. Pritchard, ed., *Ancient Near Eastern Texts* (Princeton: Princeton University Press, 1950), p. 428.

it, and to direct a report to one who has sent him, in order to
direct him to the ways of life, to make him prosper upon earth.[2]

The "teaching" had a very practical purpose. The youth who
served in the Egyptian court needed to be trained in character
and in efficiency for the duties of court life. The requisite
knowledge and moral character were to be transmitted and
learned: honesty, diligence, reliability, self-control. The ideal
person is the one who controls himself in all respects: tongue,
temper, and appetite. In contrast stands the rash and impetuous
person, the "hot-tempered man." The biblical ideals were
similar, as can be seen from Prov 14:17, 29; 15:18; 22:24-25;
29:22. The person with self-control was not simply one who
adopted this course for gain or ease. Scholars are generally
agreed that this was not a form of pragmatism (or eudaimon-
ism). The Egyptians believed that by such wholesome action a
person was integrated with the divine order of things, called
ma'at, or "justice" (it is almost untranslatable). In addition to
being divinized as a goddess, *ma'at* is the divinely established
order in creation, with which humans must live in harmony.
This is the basis of human well-being, as ordained by God, and
integration with this order is the goal of the instructions.

One of the most remarkable parallels between the Egyptian
and Israelite wisdom is "The Instruction of Amenemopet,"[3]
which is similar to Prov 22:17–24:22. Scholarly opinion, with
few exceptions, considers the Proverbs passage dependent on
the Egyptian text. The opening of Amenemopet resembles
Prov 22:17-18; it reads, "Give thy ears, hear what is said, / Give
thy heart to understand them. / To put them in thy heart is
worth while."[4] The "thirty" houses or chapters of the Egyptian

[2]*Ibid.,* p. 421.
[3]*Ibid.,* pp. 421-24.
[4]*Ibid.,* p. 421.

text is hinted at in Prov 22:20: "Have I not written for you the 'thirty'?" (slightly emended reading). The advice to avoid a hot-headed man is reflected in "Do not associate to thyself the heated man, / Nor visit him for conversation."[5] These comparisons serve to illustrate the relationship. However, the dependence of the Hebrew writer was by no means servile; he goes his own way, even while he utilized the "Thirty" of the Egyptian.

As in Mesopotamia, there are also some Egyptian writings that reflect on life and confront the inevitable question of human struggle. Of course in this they are reminiscent of Job and Qoheleth. The "Harper's Songs" complain about the shortness and sadness of life, and end up by recommending the pleasure at hand before death arrives.[6] "A Dispute Over Suicide," or "The Man Who Was Tired of Life,"[7] is an argument between a man and his own soul. He rejects all the pleasures suggested by his *ka* or soul, and finally resigns himself to death.

4. Characteristics of Wisdom Literature

Modern scholarship has succeeded in pointing out several features of Wisdom Literature which deserve treatment here. These are part of the scholarly assumptions that we are reviewing, and they can profitably orient the reader toward a more perceptive understanding of the literature. Some of these characteristics, it will be seen, are more firmly based than others.

A. The Absence of Reference to Salvation History

This is perhaps the most striking feature of biblical wisdom. There is practically no mention of the promises to the

[5]*Ibid.*, p. 423. (Cf. Prov 22:24)
[6]*Ibid.*, p. 467.
[7]*Ibid.*, pp. 405-7.

patriarchs, Exodus, covenant, Sinai, Torah ("Law"), and other aspects of salvation history. One may rightly claim that Sirach 44–50 ("the praise of the fathers") and Wisdom 10–19 (a midrash on the plagues, largely) are exceptions. But they are late books and prove the rule, so to speak. The rest of the books are silent on the favorite themes of the OT. Indeed, Job is explicitly identified as a non-Israelite; he is from "the land of Uz," and the three friends are also from beyond the land of Israel. Of course, they all argue in the vein and spirit of Israelite wisdom, because they are serving the purpose of the Israelite author of the book.

This fact ties in with a point we have discussed earlier, the wisdom of the ancient Near East. The wisdom heritage is international. While Israel gives it an Israelite home and expression, she keeps it separate from the historical traditions. It is only at the end of the wisdom movement that Ben Sira identifies personified Wisdom with Torah (Sirach 24).

B. Creation Theology

This summary statement is aligned with the previous point. If the sages did not intrude the events of their sacred history into their considerations, it was because they adhered to the perspective of international wisdom, which is that of the created world and the experience of it. God is very much a part of this perspective, and Yahweh is the only God that Israel (and the sages) rightfully acknowledged. But the sages view the Lord primarily as creator, not as covenant partner. He is celebrated frequently in the Psalms as creator. Indeed his creative activity is seen as the basis for his kingship (e.g., Psalms 93, 96, 98). In Job the Lord has recourse to creation, to let it speak for him: "Where were you when I laid the foundation of the earth? . . . Has the rain a father, / or who has begotten the drops of dew?" (Job 38:4, 28). The sages constantly probe nature for its secrets and its lessons: "Three things are too wonderful for me; / four I do not understand: / the way of an eagle in the sky, / the way of a serpent on a rock, / the way of a ship on the high seas, / and the way of a man with a maiden" (Prov 30:18-19). The mysteries of nature were thus a mirror of the mysteries of human existence. Israel was in dialogue with her environment, from which many lessons could be derived: diligence from the ant (Prov 6:6-8); the wisdom of the small—ants, badgers, locusts, and lizards (Prov 30:24-28); the birds of the air that carry one's words (Eccl 10:20). The foundation of this dialogue has been seen in Gen 1:28: "God blessed them, and God said to them, 'Be fruitful and multiply, and fill the earth and subdue it; and have dominion . . . over every living thing that moves upon the earth.'" Wisdom thought worked under the aegis of the divine blessing, and "dominion" expressed itself in drawing out parallels and lessons from nature.

Gerhard von Rad has gone so far as to say, "The experiences of the world were for her [Israel] always divine experiences as well, and the experiences of God were for her experiences of the world."[8] This is a correct and profound insight into Israel's wisdom. A distinction between the secular (or worldly) and the religious is not to be discerned in wisdom sayings which speak about earthy experience as opposed to those which mention the "Lord." (See the alternation of sayings in Prov 16:7-12.) A proverb is not religious just because it mentions the Lord. It is religious because the sages' world view is ultimately rooted in the Lord. "The fear of the Lord is the beginning of wisdom" (Prov 9:10a). It is important to appreciate this deeply religious approach to reality. Israel did not separate faith from knowledge (as we do), any more than she distinguished between the primary causality of God (who causes everything) and secondary causality.

[8]Gerhard von Rad, *Wisdom in Israel* (Nashville: Abingdon, 1972), p. 62.

C. A Search for Order

It is widely thought that biblical wisdom can be characterized as a search for order, the order that exists in nature and also in human society. This order is something that can be discovered by experience, and it is expected that one should conform to it. It would appear that such an attitude was simply a basic part of the Israelite world view. Thus Isaiah can indict Israel in terms of breaking an order implicit in the created world:

> "The ox knows its owner,
>   and the ass its master's crib;
> but Israel does not know,
>   my people does not understand." (Isa 1:3)

Amos points to an "order" to show how disorderly Israel can be:

> Do horses run upon rocks?
>   Does one plow the sea with oxen?
> But you have turned justice into poison
>   and the fruit of righteousness into wormwood. (Amos 6:12)

Hence, an order, perceptible in nature, exists, and the sages were aware of it and sought to capture it in their wisdom. As von Rad puts it,

> Thus here, in proverbial wisdom, there is faith in the stability of the elementary relationships between man and man, faith in the similarity of men and of their reactions, faith in the reliability of the orders which support human life, and thus, implicitly or explicitly, faith in God who put these orders into operation.[9]

[9]*Ibid.*, pp. 62-63.

In this respect one may agree that there is common to most peoples a basic trust in the regularity of nature and in God. However, one can still ask if a "search for order" is not rather *our* reconstruction of what the Hebrew sages were about. Perhaps we may say that they put order into the varied experiences which confronted them, order into chaos as it were. But it is not clear that they conceived of an order, a cosmos, outside of themselves as an object of search. "Coping with life," not "mastery of life," seems a more accurate description of the goal of the sages who remained aware of life's mysteries.

D. *The Kerygma of Wisdom: Life*

If the term, "kerygma," denotes primarily the proclamation of the good news as this is found in the NT, one can conceive also of a kerygma for the Wisdom Literature. The proclamation is: life! The kerygmatic aspect of wisdom is particularly prominent in Proverbs 1–9, where personified Wisdom is portrayed as preaching in the streets (1:20; 8:2; 9:3). Job's complaint is that he has no life that is worthy of the name; he could wish for respite in Sheol in order to escape the heavy hand of God that is upon him. Ecclesiastes' grief is that life is vanity, vanity of vanities. But in Proverbs a very positive view is offered by the sages: "the wage of the righteous leads to life" (Prov 10:16*a*); "he who is steadfast in righteousness will live" (11:19*a*). The practical equivalence of wisdom (*ḥokmāh*) and righteousness (*ṣedāqāh*) is clearly indicated here. To heed admonition is a "path to life" (10:17; cf. 2:19; 5:6). Again, "the teaching of the wise is a fountain of life" (13:14*a*). Wisdom herself is "a tree of life to those who lay hold of her" (3:18*a*). Hence it is no surprise to hear personified Wisdom call out, "He who finds me finds life / and obtains favor from the Lord" (Prov 8:35).

What is this "life" concretely? It is not merely length of days, a typically biblical sign of divine approval, but the quality of life: "riches and honor and life" (Prov 22:4). It is all the blessing that Job described "when God watched over me" (Job 29:2), "when my steps were washed with milk, / and the rock poured out for me streams of oil! / . . .my roots spread out to the waters, / with the dew all night on my branches, / my glory fresh with me, / and my bow ever new in my hand" (29:6, 19-20). Implicit in this is also a right relationship to God; "life" is a blessing from him. Hence this is far from being "materialism," although material possessions loom large.

"Life" can be illustrated even better from its opposite, "death." Death is catastrophic for the unwise, the wicked, because death catches them unawares and separates them from the possessions in which they trusted. For such, life is short (Prov 10:27). It is important for the modern reader to understand the dynamic notion of death in the Bible. Death is personified as a *power* which enters into the daily existence of a human being. To the extent that one experiences sickness and distress, the evils of the human condition—to that extent death is *exerting* its power. To the degree that one experiences nonlife, one is dead or "in Sheol." Hence the psalmist cries out joyfully to the Lord, "thou has brought up my soul from Sheol, restored me to life" (Ps 30:3). The language is metaphorical: a transformation of one's existence from darkness into light, from death into life.

Life and death—these realities are central, not only to the Wisdom Literature, but to the entire Bible. The careful reader will make connections between wisdom and the Deuteronomic challenge and promise: "See, I have set before you this day life and good, death and evil . . . blessing and curse; therefore choose life, that you and your descendants may live" (Deut 30:15, 19). The sages as well as the Deuteronomists had a message about life.

One might sum up the claim of traditional wisdom in a formula: Wisdom (righteousness) = Life (the good life). This formula is challenged by the author of the Book of Job and is denied by Qoheleth. But another sage recognized that the formula was in the right direction, although it required revision. The author of the Wisdom of Solomon makes an astounding statement: "righteousness is immortal" (1:15; this text will be examined in chapter 3). According to this writer, the equation is to be rewritten: Wisdom (righteousness) = Life (eternal). The point is that life with God is not viewed in terms of a body that will rise again, or a soul that will keep on living forever. Rather, eternal life is rooted in the wise and righteous life that one lives on earth. Israel had always known that "the Lord . . . brings down to Sheol and raises up" (1 Sam 2:6), but it is only at the end of the OT period that a breakthrough concerning life with God after death occurs.

E. The Limits of Wisdom

When one reads the Book of Proverbs it is easy to be seduced by its optimism. Wisdom (read also: righteousness) brings life and prosperity; folly (read also: sin) brings ruin. Did the sages really believe this?

Some scholars claim that there is an "act-consequence" mentality behind the sages' view of reality. That is to say, they saw an intimate, indeed mechanical, connection between an action and its result; if it is good, good will result; if it is evil, evil will result. This view may lurk behind such statements as Prov 26:27: "He who digs a pit will fall into it, / and a stone will come back upon him who starts it rolling." One may suspect, at first, that a profound view of reality is at work here. Is evil essentially a corruptive thing, mechanically carrying destruction within it? Does good flow over automatically into a blessing which it produces? However, just as clearly, and also more frequently, the good/evil results of human action are viewed by the sages under the aegis of divine causality. The Lord is described as rewarding good and punishing evil. He *reacts* to good and evil, favorably and unfavorably (Prov 15:29; 16:4, 7). When Job is afflicted, he knows who is to blame: not a mechanical order, but God (Job 9:22-24). On balance it may be that the "act-consequence" mentality and the view of divine intervention are both at work in the thought of the ancient Israelite. But the understanding of the all-pervasive divine causality seems to dominate biblical thought.

It would be a serious mistake to accept the world view of the sages as monolithic. Even when the sages seem most dogmatic (and teaching begets a certain dogmatic quality in the teacher), they are not unaware of the complexity of life. Embedded in the very "traditional" teaching of Proverbs 1–9 is the reminder:

My son, do not despise the Lord's discipline
    or be weary of his reproof,
for the Lord reproves whom he loves,
    as a father the son in whom he delights.   (3:11-12)

This admonition recognizes that human beings are often confronted by a mysterious God whose dealings with them are not to be stereotyped.

The early sages do not explicitly address the problem of their own limitations. But their awareness appears in many sayings. They are particularly conscious of the mystery of God which they constantly confront:

No wisdom, no understanding, no counsel,
    can avail against the Lord.   (Prov 21:30)

God is simply incalculable. A person may think that his ways are "right in his own eyes, but the Lord weighs the heart" (Prov 21:2). Again, "a man's steps are ordered by the Lord; / how then can man understand his way?" (Prov 20:24). Wisdom itself has the power to deceive a person:

> Do you see a man who is wise in his own eyes?
> There is more hope for a fool than for him.
>
> (Prov 26:12; cf. 3:7)

But it remained for the author of Job and Qoheleth to underscore the limitations, even the "failure" of wisdom. In Job 28 one learns that the human industry and ingenuity that is able to find precious minerals in the earth cannot find wisdom. The reason is simple: wisdom is with God. Qoheleth wrestles with the problem of wisdom in more dramatic fashion. He was not able to recognize any advantages for the wise man over the fool: "How the wise man dies just like the fool!" (Eccl 2:16b). Although folly is not a viable option for him, wisdom fails to bring the security it promises. He relates sadly, "I said, 'I will be wise'; but it was far from me" (7:23). Qoheleth seized on the unknown and the uncertain in the wisdom enterprises and pushed them beyond human limits. Human beings simply cannot understand the "work of God" (3:11; 7:13; 8:17; 11:5). He remains sovereignly free, beyond human standards of justice or priests.

F. The Many Faces of Wisdom

Wisdom *(ḥokmāh)* is used to designate the practical skill of an artisan, such as Bezalel, who works on the construction of the tabernacle (Exod 35:30–36:1). Such skill can be applied to various trades, even to government officials such as Ahithophel, David's counselor (2 Samuel 16–17). Wisdom is also cleverness in coping with a situation, such as is evidenced by small but wise animals (Prov 30:24-28). Coping with life (*taḥbulôt,* or "steering"; Prov 1:5) is the heart of the wise teaching given in the Book of Proverbs. This is experiential wisdom, which issues in practical commands and admonitions for human beings. Many times this is equivalent to a code of ethics.

However, the sharpest contrast is between wisdom as a divine gift and also something acquired by human industry; as something of divine origin and also terribly human. Janus-faced wisdom appears in Proverbs 1–9. Here personified Wisdom addresses Israelites with both threats and cajolery in order to persuade them to obey her and thus be blessed with the insight, power, and life that she brings (Proverbs 8). She is actually in pursuit of human beings, addressing them in public. On the other hand, there is the recognition that the insight of wisdom is not easily obtained. The sage's words betray anxiety that the offer of wisdom will be spurned by the slack reaction of human beings:

> Do not forget, and do not turn away
>   from the words of my mouth.
>   Get wisdom; get insight. . . .
> The beginning of wisdom is this: Get wisdom,
>   and whatever you get, get insight.   (Prov 4:5, 7)

At the same time, however, wisdom is begotten of God, is divine (Prov 8:22-31), a gift of God (Prov 2:6). According to Job 28 wisdom is "not found in the land of the living" (v 13), because it is with God (vv 23–27). In Sirach 24 Wisdom describes her origins from the Lord and a search for a resting place; then at the Lord's bidding she makes her dwelling in Israel and ministers to him in the Holy tabernacle. For Sirach, wisdom is Torah (Law) (24:3-23). Finally Wisdom does not come of herself; she is to be obtained by prayer, as Solomon is represented as saying in Wis 8:21–9:4a:

> But I perceived that I would not possess wisdom unless God
> gave her to me— . . .
> so I appealed to the Lord and besought him,
> and with my whole heart I said:
> "O God of my fathers and Lord of mercy, . . .
> give me the wisdom that sits by thy throne."

It may be helpful for the reader to think of these aspects of wisdom, divine and human, as divine summons and human response. From the point of view of Wisdom's divine origin, she speaks for God, inviting men to life. From the other point of view, wisdom is also that response which human beings are to make to the summons by their wise conduct.

G. The Authority of Wisdom

One must distinguish various levels of authority expressed in the Wisdom Literature. Some of the commands and prohibitions of the sages are as straightforward as the Decalogue itself. In Proverbs 3 and 22–24 one has the feeling that life and death issues are at stake. The backdrop of Sinai or a liturgical celebration is not present, but no one can mistake the authoritative tone of the sage. When personified Wisdom delivers her speeches (Proverbs 1, 8, 9), there is an unmistakable ring of divine authority.

On the other hand, many of the sayings recognize that there are ambiguities in life experiences. Riches can be a sign of divine blessing ("prosperity rewards the righteous" Prov 13:21), but "better is a dinner of herbs where love is than a fatted ox and hatred with it" (Prov 15:17). Poverty can be due to a lack of diligence (Prov 10:4), but poverty is preferable to pride (Prov 16:19). Such sayings summon the listener to test out a situation, and hence the truth of the proverb. If the saying is merely experiential, it is one's own experience that is to verify it:

> Hope deferred makes the heart sick,
> but a desire fulfilled is a tree of life.   (Prov 13:12)

It is helpful in the matter of authority to distinguish between theory and practice. In theory the authority of the sage should rank below that of the prophet. The latter proclaimed the word of the Lord ("Thus says the Lord . . ."). The sage had no divine call or mission to appeal to. Although some of them indicate certain spiritual experiences (e.g., Eliphaz in Job 4:12-21), their appeal is to experience, the way things have always been, or to examples from the created world which bear out their point. Sometimes the motives they offer seem simply pragmatic (Prov 3:9-10). The prophets, too, have recourse to various motives and advance many examples (Isa 28:23-29), but underlying their message was a divine authority.

Yet in practice the authority of the prophet may well have ranked below that of the sage, if one may judge from the reaction of Israel to prophets like Isaiah who did have an apparently small coterie of disciples (Isa 8:16), or Jeremiah who spent considerable time in stocks, in house arrest, and in jail (Jer 20:2; 36:5; 37:15). It would seem that the prophets gained more acceptance after they died, when their oracles were truly appreciated and collected for the sake of the community. Because the sages appealed to tradition and experience, without a direct divine threat, they may have gained more acceptance than the prophets.

H. The Literary Dress of Wisdom

The sages considered it important to express their views in attractive language—the right word at the right time. A certain aesthetic quality was desirable: "pleasant speech increases persuasiveness" (Prov 16:21); "pleasant words are like a honeycomb, / sweetness to the soul and health to the body" (16:24); "a word fitly spoken / is like apples of gold in a setting of silver" (25:11). The editor of Ecclesiastes wrote of Qoheleth that he "sought to find pleasing words" (12:10). While Hebrew style retains its own secrets that will not yield to translation into English, the reader of Hebrew wisdom will be well advised to take note of certain typical features.

There is a bag of literary tricks that cannot be easily reproduced in translation. These include paronomasia, assonance, and alliteration. On the other hand, one striking feature will always be clear: parallelism.

The standard characteristic of all Hebrew poetry is the parallelism of the lines. This is a thought rhythm, not a vowel rhythm as is characteristic of poetry in English. The three classical types were first treated extensively in 1753 by the Anglican bishop, Robert Lowth. He defined parallelism as a certain equality of similarity between two parts of a sentence. The words in each part correspond to each other and the thoughts match in some way.

> Have mercy on me, O God, according to thy steadfast love;
> according to thy abundant mercy blot out my transgressions.
>
> (Ps 51:1)

In this *synonymous* parallelism the second line repeats the idea of the first line. *Antithetic* parallelism presents a contrast between the two lines, but in such fashion that both lines say the

same thing, despite the negation. It is characteristic of Proverbs
10–15.

> A wise son makes a glad father,
>> but a foolish son is a sorrow to his mother.   (Prov 10:1)

Lowth called a third type *synthetic* parallelism. This is a
catch-all category for the parallelism which cannot be
conveniently classified as synonymous or antithetic. The
meaning of this category is that the first line creates a sense of
expectation which is completed in the second (or the third):

> He knows the way that I take;
>> when he has tried me, I shall come forth as gold.   (Job 23:10)

Further details about Hebrew parallelism could be spelled out,
but this will suffice here. The reader will experience much aid to
interpretation by paying attention to this device. If one line is
obscure, light is often shed on it by the parallel line.

The word that is commonly translated as "proverb" is
mashal. But the Hebrew term is used much more widely than
this English equivalent. For example, it designates a satirical
song (Isa 14:4). Moreover, "proverb" is a very difficult term to
define for any culture. Broadly speaking, it indicates a pithy,
succinct saying, based on experiential observation. For the
saying to be truly proverbial it must gain currency among a
community. Such sayings occur throughout the Bible: "out of
the wicked comes forth wickedness" (1 Sam 24:13); "what has
straw in common with wheat?" (Jer 23:28). When these sayings
take root among the people, they are passed on, and even
modified.

It would be very difficult to point out any of the sayings in the
Book of Proverbs as "proverbs" in the above sense. We are in

no position to prove that the book contains sayings that originated among and were transmitted by the people. It is just as possible that the sayings are to be attributed to teachers or sages; but of course they would naturally have been influenced by popular sayings. Some sayings were doubtless created by the sages themselves. It is interesting to note that some sayings have one line in common—a variant second line has been worked out:

> A rich man's wealth is his strong city;
>> the poverty of the poor is their ruin.   (Prov 10:15)

> A rich man's wealth is his strong city;
>> and like a high wall protecting him.   (Prov 18:11)

The wisdom saying is normally a two-line composition in parallelism, and it is based on experience. If it is merely observational, it leaves any practical conclusion up to the reader. In itself, it merely "tells it the way it is." It registers facts, as in Prov 19:6,

> Many seek the favor of a generous man,
>> and every one is a friend to a man who gives gifts.

These observational sayings express no moral, although they will point out certain ambiguities in human conduct. For example, silence is an ambiguous sign. From one point of view it can suggest a knowledgeable, careful person whose words break the silence in order to say something significant. On the other hand, there is the person whose silence is an indication of having nothing to say (Prov 17:27-28). These observations are thus open to verification; they challenge the listener to test them as indicators of reality. They are not *directly* didactic; although they do instruct the listener about reality, they do not inculcate a particular value. Their didactic character rather derives from the total context in which they are placed.

The truly didactic sayings go beyond observation, while being based on it. They definitely inculcate a particular value, and this is sometimes indicated by the "loaded" terms that are used, such as the wise (just) and foolish (wicked) contrasts that abound in Proverbs 10. The presupposition is that no one will want to identify with the fool or wicked person. A course of action may be defined in relationship to God (e.g., Prov 14:11; 19:17; 22:22-23), and such a saying does not leave any option to the hearer. This aspect is all the more emphasized when the form of the saying is expressed by an imperative instead of the usual declarative mood:

> Commit your work to the Lord,
>   and your plans will be established.   (Prov 16:3)
> He who gives heed to the word will prosper,
>   and happy is he who trusts in the Lord.   (Prov 16:20)

Both of these sayings make essentially the same point, but the imperative carries greater intensity. Other examples are Prov 10:1 and 23:22; 14:31; 22:22. The imperative mood can be expressed in a positive command or in a negative admonition. The use of the imperative mood is typical of the genre of instruction employed by the sage. The command and the prohibition can be in antithetic parallelism (Prov 8:33). Often a motive clause will be introduced to strengthen the point, as is frequent in Prov 22:17–24:34, the section that is related to the Egyptian wisdom of Amenemopet, and also in Proverbs 1–4. The use of motive clauses suggests the exercise of reflection, the intent to persuade and convince.

Thus far we have been describing various aspects of the sayings as these appear in discrete, separate, fashion in

Proverbs 10 and as also scattered in the other books. But the sages also cultivated longer, consecutive pieces. These wisdom poems appear in Proverbs 1–9, and may be called "instructions," since they are presented by a "teacher" to "my son," and thus resemble the Egyptian *Sebayit*. The genre of instruction is further characterized by commands, prohibitions, and motive clauses. Within the instructions of Proverbs 1–9 are contained "wisdom speeches," in which personified Lady Wisdom speaks publicly to an audience (1:20-33; 8; 9:1-6). The sages also cultivated the "numerical saying" in which a given number is announced (often in a graded way, x and x plus 1), and a series of phenomena are listed (cf. Proverbs 30). Another feature is the acrostic poem, in which each verse begins with the successive letters of the Hebrew alphabet, as can be seen in the poem about the ideal housewife in Prov 31:10-31.

The Book of Job has been rightly praised as a literary masterpiece. It weaves together many literary genres: the complaints, wisdom sayings, legal arguments, and hymns. These are the components of the disputes which take place in the dialogue between Job and his three "friends" (3–31).

Characteristic of the book of Ecclesiastes is the "reflexion," which has a rather loose structure. It is characterized by an observation (phrases like "I saw," 1:14; 2:13, 24, etc.), personal thought ("I said to myself," 1:16-17; 2:1, 15, etc.), and various kinds of conclusions ("There is nothing better . . . than . . . , 2:24, etc.). Ecclesiastes also makes use of several wisdom sayings (7:1-13; 10:1-20).

Sirach or the Book of Ecclesiasticus, is a veritable compendium of topics and forms: family life, friends, table manners, medicine, gossip—a bewildering array of subjects. Similarly variable are the forms that are used: wisdom sayings in the style of Proverbs 10 (10:31 13:26, etc.), instructions combining commands and prohibitions to one who is called "my son" (2:1; 3:1; 4:1, etc.), hymns 16:26–17:24; 42:15–43:33), and prayers (36:1-17).

I. Conclusion

The preceding pages have attempted to present the commonly accepted views of scholarly research. Some of these are more certain than others, but all of them help us read the texts of the Wisdom Literature with a greater understanding of their origins, goals, and style. The fruits of this historical-critical methodology, as valuable as they are, constitute only the beginning of the process of interpretation in which the modern reader is summoned to engage. There remains another aspect that must be considered: the presuppositions of the interpreter(s).

II. INTERPRETATION

In the preceding chapter we discussed the presuppositions which have emerged from the scholarly study of the Wisdom Literature. These conclusions are not all on the same level of certainty. Yet they serve as roughly accurate guides to the literal historical meaning of these ancient texts. This approach is aimed at answering the question, What *did* the text mean? In this chapter we will discuss another set of presuppositions which are more personal or existential. They are geared to answering the question, What *does* the text mean? How does it apply to the reader? The following remarks refer to reading the Bible as such, not merely to a particular portion. But the examples will be drawn largely from the Wisdom Literature.

The success of modern biblical scholarship brought with it a certain insensitivity to the exegetical works of the past. This is understandable. The new insights deriving from archaeological investigation, from comparisons with newly discovered ancient literature (think of the Babylonian creation epic *[Enuma Elish]* and the waves it created in the nineteenth century concerning its relationship to Genesis 1!), contributed to making us think that we had passed into a new age where nothing would be the same in biblical interpretation. The goal of the historical-critical method—the establishment of the meaning of the ancient text for the ancients—has been foremost, and still remains important, in biblical investigation. The astonishing number of new and independent translations in recent decades bears witness to the success of a more sophisticated knowledge of Hebrew grammar and textual tradition attained by means of modern scholarship.

This development was inevitable perhaps, and all to the good; and it will continue. At the same time many scholars, and particularly the Believing Community, have perceived the growing chasm between what the text meant "back then," and what it means "now." It is increasingly felt that the scholarly task has to engage itself on both sides of meaning, and not merely confine itself to the historical meaning of the past. Moreover, the interesting issue was raised: How many meanings does an ancient text have? Is the historical meaning of the past the only valid meaning? Is there a plus meaning inherent in the ancient text that is reached by the modern reader in a valid way? These questions receive an affirmative answer in the history of interpretation of the Bible. It is a matter of historical fact that interpreters of the Bible have consistently gone beyond the past historical meaning of a biblical text to find a meaning for their own day.

The interpretation of the literature of the past, whether secular or religious, is a very complex activity. It is not simply a question of reading a text and saying, "It means thus and so." The history of the interpretation of any given text is proof of this. In actual fact, different meanings have been honestly attached to the same book or part of a book. Such history catches us up into the process of interpretation, or hermeneutics, and makes us ask what we are really doing when we interpret a biblical text.

In modern times we have become acutely aware of the historical distance that separates us from the past, and of the meaning of an ancient text when it was written, and what it means now. The gap between what it meant and what it means is not easily closed. The difficulties are not only on the side of the contemporary meaning of the ancient text. One has to admit that the goal of historical-critical methodology can be only *approximated.* It is not possible for the modern reader to strip self of certain inevitable presuppositions and enter totally into the meaning of an ancient text. One remains a person of the twentieth century, not a citizen of Jerusalem in the time of Qoheleth. The most one can hope for is a certain clarity about what the author of Job and Ecclesiastes meant.

Assuming that one has achieved this basic clarity, how does one come to the meaning the ancient text has for today? The posing of this question flows from two undeniable facts. First, every piece of literature has an afterlife. The meaning it had for its audience and generation yields to the further meanings it carries for successive generations who read it in a new light. This is true of *any* literature, the Bible included. Perhaps the most relevant example for us is the manner in which the Constitution of the United States has been interpreted and applied since it was first adopted. This ongoing process is the closing of the gap between "then" and "now." Second, the history of biblical interpretation is a concrete illustration of how later generations, both Jewish and Christian, have discovered a meaning in the OT that goes beyond the literal historical meaning.

The theoretical investigation of this process belongs to the philosophy of hermeneutics or interpretation (what does the act of interpretation involve?). We will not discuss this, but rather focus attention on two areas: (1) the assumptions which a modern reader may bring to the reading of the biblical text;

(2) examples from the history of biblical exegesis. Discussion of these two aspects of biblical interpretation will alert us to our own presuppositions and to how they affect our understanding the OT.

1. The Presuppositions of a Modern Reader

By these presuppositions we mean certain understandings that arise not from the text but from ourselves, the particular background that forms us. These will differ with each reader, but it will be useful to describe the general forms that these presuppositions take. It is very important for every reader of the Bible to become aware of and to identify these influences, to know the presuppositions with which one is working. This will be done first in a theoretical manner by discussing a large range of issues that influence one's approach to the Bible. The purpose is not to *prescribe* certain presuppositions for the reader to adopt. Rather, it is more important simply to point these out. When we are *aware* of these, we are in a position to judge their validity. But the judgment of validity is ultimately the task of the individual reader. Doubtless the presuppositions of the present writer will inevitably come to the fore; they can be considered a challenge to the reader.

Needless to say, this chapter cannot possibly discuss all the aspects of hermeneutics involved in reading the Bible. It will deal with several, but the main purpose will be served if it produces an awareness of the hidden agenda that is often brought to the process of understanding and approaching a biblical passage.

1. One of the most powerful sets of presuppositions is the cultural baggage that we carry around with us when we attempt to interpret literature. Tradition and language have molded the way in which we understand words and metaphors and literary genres. There are certain theological and philosophical notions

that we take for granted and that we easily assume are part of the thought world of the ancient biblical writer.

Many of the differences between the modern and the biblical perception of reality will be pointed up in the interpretation of particular texts in a later chapter. Here we will merely give one illustration. Whether or not one actually believes in the existence of and the distinction between body and soul, the distinction between the two remains in modern thought patterns. When we read the word "soul" in the Bible (cf. Ps 104:1), we tend to interpret it according to our Greek heritage as distinct from the body, as being of a spiritual nature, even immortal. The issue is not whether this view is correct, but rather whether it matches the view of the biblical writers. It does not. Israel conceived of the human being as matter breathed upon by the Lord; the biblical writer did not operate with categories of body and soul. Hence the reader must beware of reading into biblical terms the content which we today attach to these terms. Even if a translation carries the word "soul," this is not meant in the same sense in which we understand it; it most often means self or person. Several other instances of this kind could be listed (e.g., Sheol), but this is not the place for it. There are many books which clarify the biblical understanding of reality (e.g., H. W. Wolff, *Anthropology of the Old Testament,* Fortress Press, 1974), and they will serve both to instruct the modern reader, as well as produce an awareness of the cultural baggage that may form our presuppositions in reading the Bible.

2. Everyone brings to the Bible some set of presuppositions of a religious (or irreligious) nature. The common attitude is that the Bible is somehow a communication from God. Thus it has been called the word of God, inspired, normative for a community. These notions are explained in different ways, and it is not possible to discuss these here. Again, what is important

is the awareness of them and of how they may influence our interpretation. The following sets of questions are designed to force the reader to come to terms with these presuppositions:

a) What is the meaning of "word of God," or "inspiration of the Holy Spirit?" Has the community of faith to which one belongs expressed any understanding of this or judgment on it?

b) What are the implications of question *a?* Many draw the conclusion that the Bible is inerrant, that it contains no error, because God is the "author" of the Bible. The assumption behind inerrancy is that God would communicate only truth (to state the issue positively). Does this mean that the Bible contains all kinds of truths, relative to natural science, history, morality, and the conception of God? Or is it legitimate to expect only that truth which is pertinent for the religious life of those who make up the Believing Community? In a similar way, one may ask if there are tensions and conflicting points of view expressed in the Bible. How can these be understood in the light of a presupposition concerning "inspiration" and "inerrancy"? Are they to be harmonized and homogenized so as to remove the conflict? We shall see the importance of the principle that the Bible is to be interpreted from the Bible; this principle is true of any general body of literature produced by a community. Does its application reveal differences or sameness of opinion within the Bible?

Merely to put these questions is to remind ourselves of the centuries of dispute that have centered on them. In many religious communities they are still burning issues. But in effect they spare no reader of the Bible; each individual takes a position on them, whether or not he or she wishes to. The very denial of them already points to an assumption.

The Wisdom Literature of the OT poses some interesting questions to this issue. For example, what is the "truth" of a saying, especially when sayings are placed in deliberate contrast

(Prov 26:4-5)? What is the "truth" of the affirmation of Job's friends which are in opposition to those of Job, but largely agree with the outlook of the Book of Proverbs? Can one recognize a movement, a development here, ranging from the optimism of Proverbs to the skepticism of Qoheleth? The sages struggled with the ways of God, and there is no one part of their message that can be absolutized. It may be more fruitful to hold these books in tension with each other. No one of them says it all; between them something of the Lord's mystery and sovereignty is communicated.

Perhaps the common denominator to be found among all who read the Bible, both Christians and Jews, is that this literature at least contains something to learn, possible guidelines for thinking and living. The assumption is that the literature still has something to say to the modern reader, that it is somehow addressed to the modern person. For many it may have no more authority than the classical literature of the ancient Near East or of ancient Greece and Rome, but it is read, interpreted, and applied in the life of the individual. This itself is an assumption.

3. What effect has the historical distance that separates the modern reader from the biblical literature? In modern times interpretation of literature, especially of the Bible, has become acutely aware of the historicity of humans and their words. That is to say, each person and every word reflect the age to which they belong, and the world passes through several ages. One cannot simply transfer a statement from the ancient world into present circumstances; there is a process of hermeneutics at work that inevitably adapts and appropriates the literature of the past. What has been written in the ancient world (and in the modern as well) is time conditioned, rather than timeless. It has to be reinterpreted in the new situation of surviving ages. Hence the importance of the history of interpretation of such a

work as the Bible; one catches the hermeneutical process at work. If the message is presumed to have validity, it is still not abstracted, like a tooth, and put into a new setting. It is reinterpreted by and for the new setting.

Thus one may ask how the advice of an Israelite sage in the seventh or third centuries B.C. can be presumed to speak to a person of an entirely different culture of the twentieth century. Various presuppositions must be at work.

a) One presumes upon a basic sameness in human beings as regards their aspirations and their experiences. This continuity between then and now is all the more important in view of the obvious discontinuity of language and culture and even in the sense of values.

b) There is a presumption (of faith) that the literature gathered by the community of faith and proclaimed as its charter, so to speak, for existence, must have a bearing on the life-style of a member of that community. The consensus of the community is an important factor in the ongoing process of interpretation of the biblical message. A certain tradition forms concerning the nucleus of the message. Individual interpreters contribute in varying degrees to this process, but the permanent understanding of the biblical message (e.g., the mystery of God, the divine will for salvation, etc.) is ultimately yielded by the understanding of the faith community. The "Lone Ranger" approach results in idiosyncrasies.

c) Lines of continuity can be established between the meaning of the text in its first historical context and the further understanding and appropriation it can have in a present context. Thus, when the Israelite sages affirm the promise that wisdom brings life, there are many particularities that are implied: the particular understanding of wise conduct in their society, the "good life" of prosperity, honor, and other values that were associated with such conduct. This perspective may differ from ours. Nonetheless we can detect a certain continuity between the biblical "life" and the "life" we want to enjoy in our own situation. We can accept the principle that wisdom brings life (along with the limitations which the sages recognized in it), and we can attempt to appropriate it and expand it in the new and changed conditions in which we exist. Both wisdom and life are for us filled with components that escaped the awareness of the biblical sages, but not the reach of their vision. We accept their insights and attempt to verify them in areas that correspond to the biblical situation. If the sage made a concrete point about diligence, or poverty, or the use of the tongue, this has to be seen against the background of the Israelite society. Nonetheless the thrust of these sayings reaches us as pertinent and somehow applicable within our own perspective: we see the value of diligence over against laziness; of self-control over against dissipation. Or we participate in a sense of wonderment and awe that the sages showed in contemplating the divine creation (Proverbs 30; Job 38–41). We know the physical world in a manner different from theirs; we may even have more reasons for praising the mysteries of creation. But it is the sage who can communicate to us the sense of awe.

2. Lessons from the History of Exegesis

The history of biblical exegesis, both Jewish and Christian, is a relatively neglected area, and we can do no more here than present a few examples of Christian exegesis of Wisdom Literature. Scores of manuscript commentaries from patristic through medieval times remain unpublished. Of course, the works of the giants have been made available, and have received due attention: Jerome and Augustine in the West, Origen and the Cappadocians in the East, the midrashim and commentaries of Rashi, and other Jewish commentators. But in many cases attention to the flow of patristic, medieval, and Reformation exegesis has been little more than a curtsy. The "headiness" of the results achieved by modern biblical methods made it difficult to assess the value of ancient exegesis which labored under so many disadvantages from which the modern era had freed itself. The result has been that historical scholarship has investigated these ancient commentators and discussed mutual influences and summed up their views, and then dismissed them. The cleavage between the modern and the ancient seems too great.

Nevertheless there are both positive and negative lessons that can be drawn from the history of interpretation. The recognition of the presuppositions operative in the past is particularly valuable for modern readers who might fail to be aware of their own assumptions. The importance of this brief sketch lies mainly in the recognition of certain assumptions and how these influence the process of interpretation.

Origen (about A.D. 185-253) is one of the giants among biblical interpreters, and he wielded enormous influence on later generations. His acceptance of Solomonic authorship for Proverbs, Ecclesiastes, and the Song of Songs is an assumption that lived almost up to recent times. Along with it went a tidy understanding of what these three books were about, as we can see from the prologue to his commentary on the Song of Songs:

> First, in Proverbs he (Solomon) taught the moral science, putting rules for living into the form of short and pithy maxims, as was fitting. Secondly he covered the science known as natural in Ecclesiastes; in this, by distinguishing the useless and vain from the profitable and essential, he counsels us to forsake vanity and cultivate things useful and upright. The inspective science likewise he has propounded in this little book that we have now in hand—that is, the Song of Songs. In this he instils

into the soul the love of things divine and heavenly, using for his purpose the figure of the Bride and Bridegroom, and teaches us that communion with God must be attained by the paths of charity and love.[1]

This view was transmitted to the medieval period by Jerome in his commentary on Eccl 1:1 where he speaks of a threefold category of "beginners," "proficient," and "perfect." Thus, early on, these wisdom books are evaluated in terms of the three stages (live virtuously, reject what is vain, love God) of the spiritual growth of a Christian.

The assumption of Solomonic authorship (which Christians shared with the Jews) is not historically correct, according to today's scholarly judgment. Authorship is a very delicate claim in the area of biblical writings. It is more important to realize that we are ignorant of the identity of authors of much of the OT and to leave it an open question. Otherwise, we can find ourselves in the constricted position of Origen and others. There is a tendency to systematize the writings if they are attributed to one man (e.g., the "psalms of David"), and thus put them in a limited, if not false, perspective. The limitations are more important than simply an erroneous claim about authorship. One fails to see the richness of the development of the wisdom movement across Israel's history when Proverbs is fitted into the life span of King Solomon. Similarly, Qoheleth's dialogue with his time (the Hellenistic period of the third century) is missed if the book is shifted back to the tenth century. In other words, such assumptions about authorship can be crippling.

On the other hand, there is a kind of existential thrust to the attempt to correlate these books with the life of the believer.

[1]Cf. Origen, *The Song of Songs: Commentary and Homilies,* trans. R. P. Lawson (Westminster, Md.: Newman Press, 1957), p. 41.

The effort of Origen is correct in its basic hermeneutical thrust. For the needs of the community he was serving, he utilized his immense learning (immense for his time) to be practical and relevant.

Origen was far more than a preacher; he was a sophisticated philosopher and theologian as well. While this training broadened his approach to the Bible, it also led him into certain presuppositions which today we would not consider tenable. In his great work *On First Principles* he raises questions about the meaning of the biblical text that are very modern. At the same time he recognized three meanings, in harmony with body, soul, and spirit that make up a human being: the bodily or historical meaning, the psychic or moral meaning, and the pneumatic or mystical meaning. The imposition of such a grid on the biblical text leads to the recognition of multiple meanings (and Origen is modern in this respect), but very frequently a meaning is *read into* the text under the guise of "moral" or "mystical" meaning. Another principle, basic not only to Origen but also to the entire stream of Christian tradition, is that the OT speaks directly to the Christian. This obliterates the possibility of a distinction in revelation, in time, in growth, in the relationship between the two testaments. Again, the principle is in the right direction: the Christian reads the OT to draw profit from it, but initially it was not directed to the Christian community. Hence continuity, rather than identity with one's own Christian setting, should be sought for.

In his work on the Song of Songs Origen was "literal" enough to call it a "drama," and to recognize the difference in the speakers. He even proposed a concrete setting for 2:9-13 and recognized the appearance of the lover to the beloved in the spring. She had "doubtless sat indoors all winter, to come forth now, as at a fitting time." Then he comments immediately that "these things seems to me to afford no profit to the reader as far as the story goes. . . . It is necessary, therefore, to give them all a spiritual meaning." Here he gives in too easily to what he judges as being of spiritual relevance, and very often he resorts to allegory.

Sometimes a wholesale verdict is rendered on the interpretation of the past by the use of the word, "allegorical," almost in the sense of an escapist and unreal manner of interpretation. A few comments are in order. Allegory is first of all mode of writing, or composition, before it is a mode of interpretation. A given literary work is deliberately written in allegorical style, that is, the details that appear in the story are all to be given, by the author's design, a transferred meaning. An example of this is Qoheleth's description of old age in Eccl 12:3-5. It is clear from the context that he is talking about old age, but the terms he uses do not directly refer to the phenomena of old age. Thus, "keepers of the house tremble, and the strong men are bent" seems to refer to the weakness of arms and legs. If commentators differ with regard to the precise interpretation of the terms, they are almost at one in agreeing that each term has a transferred meaning. This is what the author intended to do. However, we may not assume that allegorical interpretation, seeking for transferred meanings, can be applied anywhere and everywhere; it holds good only for those particular texts, and they are quite few, that have been written in this mode.

Unfortunately many interpreters of the past indulged in this style of interpretation. Indeed, the influential Gregory the Great conceived of allegory as "a certain kind of machine" that would elevate the soul to God. Today we recognize that there are other ways of apprehending the sense of Scripture, without having recourse to a literary device which does not match the intentions of the original writer. At the same time, modern interpreters are not always innocent of the charge of allegorism.

There still exists a tendency to spiritualize the biblical text, in a one-on-one fashion, that goes contrary to its meaning.

Perhaps the most popular example of allegorical interpretation is the Song of Songs. The book serves as a test case for allegorism, and the history of its interpretation shows both the extravagances of this mode as well as the deeper meaning that the Song might have. The allegorical interpretation of the Song consists in interpreting it as a dialogue between God and his people (Israel or the church according to the respective Jewish and Christian tradition). This can bring with it an allegorical reference, that is to say, the intent of the text is to describe the relation between the Lord and his people, not the relationship between a man and a woman. The details of the text are then understood to refer to specific items that fit into the general meaning: for example, the two breasts of the woman (7:3) are said by some to be references to Mt. Ebal and Mt. Gerizim. It may be said that the whole weight of such allegorical detail gives an air of unreality to the interpretation. The references are seen as arbitrary, coming from the interpreter's fertile imaginaton rather than from the text itself.

The obvious meaning of the Song seems to be a description of the loving relationship between a man and a woman. This is love poetry in which both the man and the woman express their yearning, admiration, and affection for each other. Does this literary genre make sense in the Bible? Obviously human love is an object deserving consideration. And many scholars assume that this particular book was preserved and transmitted by the sages of Israel who recognized here a treatment of essential value to the well-being of the community. Such would be the literal historical meaning of the Song.

On the other hand, does this understanding exhaust the meaning of the book? Even if there is an exaggerated allegorism to be found in much of the Jewish and Christian literature concerning the book, is the basic insight that the work deals with divine/human love worthy of attention? Several considerations argue for the validity of this view. First of all there is the fact that human sexual love becomes a vehicle in biblical thought to understand the covenant relationship between God and people. This is particularly clear in Hosea 1–3, in which the love relationship of the prophet and his wife serves as a symbol of the relationship between the Lord and Israel. This datum is expanded in many other books of the OT (e.g., cf. Isa 62:4-5) and finds an echo in Eph 5:21-33. Second, the text at 8:6 suggests that human love can be seen in the context of divine love; the flames of human love are "the flames of Yahweh." (See the treatment of 8:6 in chapter 3.) It is not unreasonable then to recognize another level of meaning, captured in both Jewish and Christian interpretation, in the Song. It is not reached by any arbitrary mode of allegory, but from the text itself, and from the deployment of the marriage symbol within the Bible. The insight of the prophets suggests that the sexual relationship of human beings somehow reflects a divine reality. The love that they share is a participation in something divine; it is not a gratuitous symbol, but one that arose from the depths of human experience.

It is in this context that Bernard of Clairvaux can be understood and appreciated. Over a period of eighteen years (1135-1153) he composed eighty-six sermons on the Song which were delivered to the monks at the monastery of Clairvaux. He does not approach the book from the point of view of technical exegesis, nor is the allegorical method, even if it is not absent from his work, the key to the Song. He ranges far and wide across the relationship of love between an individual and God. He is a mystic who writes for those who believe that Scripture, and the Song in particular, should lead to the knowledge and love of God. In Sermon 79 we read:

Here love speaks everywhere! If anyone desires to grasp these writings, let him love! For anyone who does not love it is vain to listen to this song of love, or to read it, for a cold heart cannot catch fire from its eloquence. The one who does not know Greek cannot understand Greek, nor can one ignorant of Latin understand another speaking Latin, etc. So, too, the language of love will be meaningless jangle, like sounding brass or tinkling cymbal, to anyone who does not love."

For him the Song is the "book of experience," and the greatest experience is love. Bernard utilized the Song in such a way that it prompted and corresponded with the love with which he himself was consumed. "Dynamic equivalence" is perhaps the modern phrase that best suits his development of the point of the Song of Songs.

There are two fundamental observations that have to be kept in mind in assessing the patristic and medieval interpretation of the Bible. First, most of the expositors of the Bible were clerics (although Origen was more of a philosopher and catechist, not being ordained a priest till mid-life), because they were more educated and were capable of teaching. Second, one should respect the nature of the literary works in which these people expounded the Bible. There is a world of difference between a homily and a commentary; they are two different literary genres in our day, and no less in times past. "Commentaries," in the modern sense of the word, have never existed until the last few centuries, even if they had prototypes that go back to the medieval period. The immediate purpose of the homily, especially if within the context of a liturgical celebration, was to move the congregation to greater sensitivity to God, and also to explain an aspect of Christian faith and life. There was the naive, if beautiful, assumption that the viewpoint and thoughts of the biblical writers were identical with those of the interpreter and the audience. They were simply not aware of the problem of historical consciousness (the historical distance that separates the Bible from our own faith and theology) which has been brought home to us only in modern times.

The patristic and medieval understanding of the Song as a dialogue between God and people was maintained in Reformation exegesis as well. As was the case with Origen, Solomonic authorship was presumed. Luther described the work as "an encomium of the political order, which in Solomon's day flourished in sublime peace." In it Solomon thanks God "for that highest blessing, external peace."[2] Although he rejected the mystical approach of the medievals (God and the individual soul), this view was taken up in later Reformation commentaries. Calvin never wrote a commentary on the Song, but his views can be inferred from his strong opposition to Castellion's questioning of the canonicity and the decency of the Song. Calvin referred the Song to Christ and the church, and this ecclesiological understanding is reflected also in the works of Theodore of Beza and other Reformation commentators.

It is only within the last two centuries that the recognition of the Song as love poetry, dealing with the relationship between man and woman, has emerged. And it has attained practically unanimous approval, as the historical-critical methodology developed. This is all to the good, insofar as this meaning was never really heard in ages past. But now the challenge remains for the modern reader, as we have seen, Is it to be considered the *only* level of meaning in the Song?

In this brief sketch it is impossible to analyze all the factors that account for the change in interpretation of the Song and of the Bible generally. It is the story of human beings becoming

[2]*Luther's Works*, vol. 15, trans. Jaroslav Pelikan et al. (St. Louis: Concordia Publishing House, 1971), pp. 194-95.

conscious of their historicity. But one can point to certain key changes in the regnant presuppositions that brought about the change for the Song: the end of Solomonic authorship; recognition that the topic of sexuality is not foreign to biblical inspiration; broader sense of the historicity of an ancient text, especially in the light of the discoveries of other love poems in ancient literatures from the Fertile Crescent; the growing awareness that the OT has its own message; and its own relevance for communities of faith that adopted it.

The history of the interpretation of Ecclesiastes provides another example of the importance of the presuppositions brought to interpretation. Here also, as we have seen, presumptions of Solomonic authorship prevailed up into modern times. The striking motto of the book, "vanity of vanities! All is vanity" (Eccl 1:2) was given a particular twist, due to the eschatological beliefs of Christian commentators. Their tendency was to recognize this as a verdict on the values of this life in comparison with the glory of the next life. This perspective, of course, is totally foreign to Qoheleth, and it really takes the sting out of his words. Nonetheless it is reflected in such a famous book of popular devotion as the *Imitation of Christ* (Book 1, chapter 1). No matter the personal eschatological beliefs of the modern reader, it must be asked if Qoheleth is not better heard with all the tensions he poses to Christian beliefs. One might surmise that Dietrich Bonhoeffer could have had the Book of Ecclesiastes (cf. 9:10; 11:9) particularly in mind when he wrote, "It is only when one loves life and the earth so much that without them everything seems to be over, that one can believe in the resurrection and a new world."[3]

But the tensions recognizable in Ecclesiastes are more than those between O and NT. There are tensions within the book

[3]Dietrich Bonhoeffer, *Letters and Papers from Prison* (New York: Macmillan, 1953), p. 103.

itself. Qoheleth both praises and condemns joy as useless (2:2; 8:15); he says he loathes life (2:17), but also, "a living dog is better than a dead lion" (9:4). The ancients were inclined to regard certain passages as instances of Solomon dialoguing with his opponents (e.g., the sentiments expressed in 9:1-3). Certain views were considered to be out of harmony with "Solomon" and ascribed to someone else. This view emerges already in the third century, and Gregory the Great adopts it when he explains the name, Ecclesiastes:

> This book, then, is called "the preacher" because in it Solomon makes the feeling of the disorganized people his own in order to search into and give expression to the thoughts that come to their untutored minds perhaps by the way of temptation. For the sentiments he expresses in his search are as varied as the individuals he impersonates.

This approach is surprisingly modern, in the sense that it anticipates the views of nineteenth- and twentieth-century scholars who recognized the same tensions, but attributed the views that were in conflict with Qoheleth's skepticism to later glossators who would have inserted the opposite opinions in order to temper the sharpness of the author.

At a later period the theological concerns of the Reformation provide a background for understanding the viewpoint of John Brentius (Brenz), who composed the first commentary on Ecclesiastes to be written by a Reformer (1528). He maintains "that this book is, so to speak, an appendix to the Law of Moses. Now the Law teaches us that man of himself is utterly unable to act virtuously, and that the more he asserts himself to acquire righteousness by his own words and thoughts, the more he fails in his attempt."[4]

[4]Cf. C. D. Ginsburg, *Coheleth and Song of Songs* (New York: Ktav Publishing House, 1970), p. 111.

Luther, too, accepted Solomonic authorship, and his view was: "Solomon wants to put us at peace and to give us a quiet mind in the everyday affairs and business of this life, so that we may live contentedly in the present without care and yearning about the future."[5] It is worth noting that the principle of Solomonic authorship shaped Jewish interpretation of this book. The Targum set the tone for this, claiming that Solomon foresaw Israel's later history, the division of the kingdom and exile.

This brief essay into the history of the interpetation of some of the Wisdom Literature should give the reader a broader perspective on the way in which this literature has been interpreted. It also conveys positive and negative aspects of the modes of exegesis of the past; this is valuable for one's own examination of personal presuppositions. Whether or not one agrees with the giants of the patristic, medieval, and Reformation periods is not the point; rather, these perspectives enrich our own understanding of what it is to interpret the Bible. We should not be surprised at the nature of the presuppositions that past interpreters brought to the Bible. Rather, we should examine our own assumptions; these may very well turn out to be surprising to future generations!

[5]*Luther's Works*, 3-175.

III. SELECTIONS FROM WISDOM LITERATURE

The purpose of the preceding chapters was to alert the reader to the range of assumptions, scholarly and personal, which are often brought to the interpretation of biblical texts. Such assumptions were also illustrated from the history of biblical interpretation. In this chapter a few selected texts will be interpreted, to serve as examples. They are exemplary only in the sense that they are meant to provide a challenge as to how one might profitably go about the work of interpretation. A perusal of commentaries reveals the various approaches that have been taken by scholars. But all of these will at least go through certain fundamental steps: establishing the context of the verses to be commented on, an analysis of pertinent terms, and the statement of the meaning. These considerations will structure the exegesis in the following examples.

There are, of course, more than three moves in explaining a biblical text, but at least these three steps are basic and helpful. Several times the "meaning" is stated on different levels; that is, the literal meaning of the past is put forth as a challenge to the modern reader to adopt and adapt. Reasons of space preclude detailed analysis. The texts to be commented on have been selected with an eye to variety and importance within a given book. Thus, in the case of the passages from Job a fairly complete idea of the meaning of the book emerges.

1. Proverbs

Prov 1:7

The fear of the Lord is the beginning of knowledge;
fools despise wisdom and instruction.

Context. Verse 7 is an independent statement, to be set off from 1:2-6, which is a consecutive series of purpose clauses concerning the function of "the proverbs of Solomon" (title, v 1). Moreover, v 7 is not continued in 1:8, in which a teacher begins to address "my son" about the need to obey parental instruction.

Although there is no immediate context for v 7, the Bible itself provides a broad context. The connection between wisdom or knowledge and the fear of the Lord is affirmed again in Prov 9:10; 15:33; Ps 111:10; Job 28:28. Fear of God/Lord is obviously an important idea, and it may be asked if this saying does not call attention to itself by its peculiar position at the beginning of the book. It has the air of being a motto, set up by the editor(s).

Terms. "Fear of God/the Lord" is a fundamental concept in the Hebrew Bible, but it means different things in different books. The notion develops out of the sense of the numinous: awe before the Lord. This is particularly clear in the frequent description of the Lord and his actions by the Hebrew term, *nōrā'* ("fearsome," not "terrible"). In Deuteronomy those who "fear" the Lord are those who are faithful to his covenant. Fear, service, and love are included in the hortatory style of the writer (Deut 6:1-5). In the Psalms a communal element appears: those who fear the Lord are the worshiping community of the faithful. In the Wisdom Literature it designates proper ethical conduct, but another nuance also appears: the phrase is often associated with devotion to the Law, as in Ps 112:1, and as one would expect in Sir 19:20. One should be mindful of the range of such a phrase which has a great history within Israel's traditions.

In Prov 1:7 "fear of the Lord" is contrasted with the attitude of "fools," (thus substituting the concrete for the abstract, in the parallel line), and "knowledge" is paralleled by "wisdom and instruction." It is important to remember that knowledge or wisdom is *both* concrete action and knowledge of how to go about it. Wisdom combines practice and theory. Fear of the Lord is the "beginning" in the sense that it leads to knowledge of wisdom.

Meaning. The many forms of this saying and the frequent reference to "fear of the Lord" in the Wisdom Literature generally (cf., e.g., Prov 1:29; 2:5; 3:7) shows that it is a basic datum in the wisdom enterprise. The pursuit of wisdom is inseparable from the proper attitude toward the Lord. This is a remarkable statement, to claim that one's relationship to God is the primary fact in the pursuit of wisdom. When one knows God one is able to know all else. On this von Rad has commented:

> The thesis that all human knowledge comes back to the question about commitment to God is a statement of penetrating perspicacity. . . . It contains in a nutshell the whole Israelite theory of knowledge. . . . One becomes competent and expert as far as the orders in life are concerned only if one begins from knowledge about God. To this extent, Israel attributes to the fear of God, to belief in God, a highly important function in respect of human knowledge. She was, in all seriousness, of the

opinion that effective knowledge about God is the only thing that puts a man into a right relationship with the objects of his perception. . . . The statement that the fear of the Lord was the beginning of wisdom was Israel's most special possession.[1]

Today such a statement as Prov 1:7 is a challenge to modern persons whose knowledge has become so diversified and complex. Israel was not able to separate knowledge from action, as we have succeeded so effectively in doing. They are held together, theory and praxis, and rooted in a personal relationship to God. The unity of knowledge and wisdom, despite its complexity, is at issue. As Israel saw it, a relationship to God lies at the heart of true wisdom.

Prov 8:22-36

22   "The Lord created me at the beginning of his work,
          the first of his acts of old.
23   Ages ago I was set up,
          at the first, before the beginning of the earth.
24   When there were no depths I was brought forth,
          when there were no springs abounding with water. . . .
26   before he had made the earth with its fields,
          or the first of the dust of the world.
27   When he established the heavens, I was there,
          when he drew a circle on the face of the deep, . . .
29   when he assigned to the sea its limit,
          so that the waters might not transgress his command,
     when he marked out the foundations of the earth,
30   then I was beside him, like a master workman;
     and I was daily his delight,
          rejoicing before him always,
31   rejoicing in his inhabited world
          and delighting in the sons of men.

[1]Von Rad, *Wisdom in Israel,* pp. 67-68.

32 And now, my sons, listen to me:
    happy are those who keep my ways.
33 Hear instruction and be wise,
    and do not neglect it.
34 Happy is the man who listens to me,
    watching daily at my gates,
    waiting beside my doors.
35 For he who finds me finds life
    and obtains favor from the Lord;
36 but he who misses me injures himself;
    all who hate me love death.''

Context. This passage forms the ending of a lengthy address delivered by Wisdom "beside the gates in front of the town" to all who pass by (8:3). Before considering the context it is necessary to define what is going on here. Wisdom is personified as a woman. This is a *literary* personification, and there are many examples in the Bible: love and faithfulness meet, while righteousness and peace kiss (Ps 85:10). Truth falls in the public squares and uprightness cannot enter the city (Isa 59:14). "Wine is a mocker, strong drink a brawler" (Prov 20:1a). In a similar way, Dame Folly appears in Proverbs 9 as a counterpart to the personification of Lady Wisdom.

Wisdom is personified in Job 28, Proverbs 1, 8, 9 and in Sirach 24. A brief consideration of these passages (Sirach 24 will be considered separately) provides the broad context for understanding Proverbs 8.

The concern of Job 28 is clearly indicated by the question expressed in vv 12 and 20, "Where shall wisdom be found?" The poem begins by pointing out that the most precious objects can be found in the depths of the earth; but the way to wisdom remains unknown, whether to humans or beasts; "it is hid from the eyes of all living" (v 21). The answer is that God alone knows the way of it (v 23), because his vision extends to the ends

of the earth, everywhere (v 24). In his work at creation
(vv 25-26),

> Then he saw it and declared it;
>> he established it, and searched it out.   (28:27)

The verbs are tantalizingly vague. One can be sure that wisdom
is with God, and not to be found by humans; but also, God has
put wisdom somewhere. Wisdom is something that can be
"numbered" or declared, can be "established." But no one
except the creator knows where it is!

Sir 1:9 provides a helpful commentary on Job 28:27. For him,
"All wisdom comes from the Lord and is with him for ever"
(Sir 1:1). Before all things she was created:

> The Lord himself created wisdom;
>> he saw her and apportioned her,
>> he poured her out upon all his works.
> She dwells with all flesh according to his gift,
>> and he supplied her to those who love him.   (Sir 1:9-10)

As in Job 28, wisdom is with God, but Sirach seems to move
beyond this when he says that God has poured wisdom upon all
his works, upon all living things ("flesh"). Sirach could never
have said that wisdom is not in the world. And perhaps Job has
not said this either; it is just that Job's emphasis is that no one
can find the way to wisdom, which is ultimately with God. With
this Ben Sira agrees, when he says "the root of wisdom—to
whom has it been revealed?" (Sir 1:6a). But he develops
considerably the Joban notion (Job 28:27) that God has done
something with this mysterious wisdom. In 1:2-3 Sirach
mentions several of the works of creation as beyond human
understanding: the sand of the sea, the drops of rain, heaven's
height, and earth's breadth. These are yet distinct from wisdom

which "was created before all things" (1:4) and nevertheless "poured out" (1:9) by God upon his works. The understanding of these passages is as mysterious as wisdom itself. But at least there seems to be a basis for distinguishing wisdom and the works of creation. They are not simply identifiable; yet wisdom is a divine quality, something present within them, a gift from God. Indeed this mysterious wisdom may be the reason humans are overwhelmed by works of creation; it is a divine quality imparted to them.

Next is the immediate context: Proverbs 1–9. In chaps. 1 and 9 Wisdom is also personified as a woman. The personification in 1:20-33 is relatively modest. Wisdom's address is pitched to those who do not seem to be enthusiastic about her, the "simple ones" who need instruction. Her brief invitation to them is followed by a very harsh motivation. She describes them as having rejected her plea (vv 24-25), and hence subject to destruction, at which Wisdom herself will merely laugh. Then even though they will invoke her, she will not respond; they will receive what they have deserved, "the fruit of their way" (vv 26-32). Only the final verse is positive: "He who listens to me will dwell secure." The threatening tone is unusually severe. Commentators have pointed out that Wisdom takes on the style of the Lord's words in Jer 7:24-27 and Isa 65:12; 66:4 (not listening when called to). Wisdom's laughing is reminiscent of the divine laughter and ridicule in Pss 2:4 and 59:8. Wisdom's refusal to hear when they finally do call is echoed from Mic 3:4; Isa 1:15; Hos 5:6. The description of the divine origins of Wisdom in chap. 8 are already prepared for this description in chap. 2.

In Proverbs 9, Lady Wisdom and Dame Folly each issue an invitation to the "simple" (9:4, 16) to turn into her house for a meal. Wisdom has prepared a banquet where her food, i.e., wisdom, can be eaten (v 5). The imagery is reminiscent of

Isa 55:1-3. Folly's offering is described pejoratively (v 17, bread and water), and the writer remarks that "her guests are in the depths of Sheol" (v 18). The contrast then is between the banquet of life and the banquet of death offered by these two speakers.

Terms. Proverbs 8 provides the main, and the longest, speech of Wisdom. She is introduced as speaking where she can expect a large audience (8:1-3), and she addresses men, even the simple and foolish who need instruction. She offers truth and righteousness, wisdom that is more precious than silver and gold. In vv 12-21 she continues to describe her qualities, association with royalty, her value and her gifts, by presenting herself in the first person, "I." The climax comes in vv 22-31 where she describes her origins.

There is the forthright statement that the Lord created (or "acquired," Hebr. *qnh*) her at the very first. In an elaborate style that is reminiscent of Egyptian and Mesopotamian creation hymns ("when there was yet no . . ."; "before . . ."), she affirms her priority before all creation. She was "set up" (better, "poured forth," Hebr. *nsk*); she was "brought forth" (the verb indicates birth)—all this before anything was created. Wisdom repeatedly describes herself as *present* when God began the preliminary actions of creation (vv 27-29). She calls herself an *'āmôn,* which has been translated in various ways: "master workman" (RSV); "darling" (NEB). It is unfortunate that we cannot determine precisely the meaning of *'āmôn;* it is impossible to be certain that it indicates Wisdom's participation in the act of creation. However, the emphasis on her *presence* is very significant, as can be inferred from Job 38:20-21. Here the Lord taunts Job about whether he was born when light and darkness were assigned their places. The implication is that if he had been born then he would be the possessor of a consummate knowledge of creation and its secrets. Hence Wisdom's emphasis on her anteriority and presence is a claim to an intimate knowledge of creation. Wisdom goes on in vv 30-31 to speak about joy and delight. She describes herself as "delight" (presumably the Lord's), and as "rejoicing before him always." By analogy we may picture her as participating in such a celebration as described in Job 38:7, when "all the sons of God shouted for joy" as the foundation of the earth was laid. The verb "rejoicing" is twice used, and it is better rendered as "playing" (Hebr. *šḥq*). Something festive is going on, as when David danced before the ark (2 Sam 6), and when "the morning stars sang together" (Job 38:7). Finally, her delight (repeated in vv 30-31) is pointed toward human beings; they bring her joy.

Meaning. What is to be made of this unusual Wisdom, born of God before any created thing, present (and hence knowledgeable) at creation, and a joy to God, and finding joy in human beings? Such a broad characterization as this makes identification difficult. The time-honored interpretation has been that Proverbs 8 merely provides a commentary on 3:19 ("The Lord by wisdom founded the earth"); that is, we have here a statement that wisdom is an attribute of God in his creative activity, an act interior to him. Somehow, this seems very flat in view of the lengthy description in 8:22-31. Of course God is wise. But is that all the poem has to say? Does it go beyond wisdom *in* God to a wisdom that is his gift to human beings in creation, a gift which is turned toward them and soliciting their adherence?

Gerhard von Rad (*Wisdom in Israel,* pp. 156-57) has rightly denied that personified Wisdom is merely an attribute of God. But he seems to divorce her from God when he characterizes her only as an attribute of the world. Wisdom seems to be too closely identified with God (Prov 8:35, "he who finds me finds life"), to be divorced from him. Rather, Wisdom is radically divine, God's gift, the divine summons issued to human beings through a creation on which God lavished his wisdom (Sir 1:9).

The implications of this for the modern reader are rather "heady." Does the Wisdom of God still speak to us through creation, or (as we shall see Ben Sira claim) through the law, or (as Paul claims, 1 Cor 1:24, 30) through Christ? Why not through all these?

Prov 12:21

No ill befalls the righteous,
    but the wicked are filled with trouble.

Context. A basic optimism floods through the Book of Proverbs: Wisdom brings life and prosperity; folly yields death and destruction (cf. 4:14-27; 10:2, 31; 11:6, and *passim*). In practice wisdom and virtue (or "righteousness," *ṣedāqāh*) are identified, as also folly and evildoing. Wisdom and folly have to do with practical affairs, how to conduct oneself. They do not say anything primarily about theoretical intelligence or the lack thereof.

This point of view is not peculiar to Proverbs. It is reflected most emphatically in Ps 37 (treated in chapter 4), where the psalmist encourages the just (wise) not to be disturbed when the fool (wicked) prospers. Things will work out for those who trust in God. He will ensure a just retribution—is he not after all a just and kind God (Exod 34:6)? Indeed, this view of retribution is central to Israelite belief, as can be seen from the stirring words in Deut 30:15-20.

We must put ourselves in the perspective of Israelite wisdom, that is to say, within the perspective of experience and observation. Does a saying such as Prov 12:21 claim that events always turn out according to this rule? There is nothing in the words that suggest any qualification. But how were such apparently absolute sayings received? It appears that several attitudes were possible.

1. Some found that this view actually worked, as a rule of thumb, so to speak. But they were also aware of the limitations of wisdom, even if these are not explicitly expressed. They often pointed to the unknown and uncalculable way of God: no human being could be master of his own way (Prov 16:9; 20:24), and against the Lord wisdom was of no avail (21:30). This also formed part of the wisdom teaching.

2. Others were not willing to admit any exceptions. These would be represented by the author of Psalms 37 and by the friends of Job. They were staunch believers in a hard and fast line of retribution.

3. Still others obviously wished to correct this view, and they did so by arguing the case for the innocent person who suffers (Job), or by pointing out the facts that contradict the theory (Ecclesiastes).

● Nonetheless it remains true that this type of saying often appears without qualification. The qualification, if there is any, has to be supplied from the various groups we have described. It is important to recognize within the Wisdom Literature (and within the Bible generally), that the absolutizing of a statement usually leads to difficulty. Situations change; revelation grows. Dialectic is at work; not only "this," but "that," also. If within Israel itself there existed more subtle and sophisticated understandings of such proverbs (as we have seen above), it ill behooves us to neglect the dialectical movement within the people by absolutizing such a saying.

Terms. These are rather clear and do not need explanation.
Interpretation. The above remarks concerning the growth in understanding, or implicit modifications in understanding the point of view of 12:21, are a warning to us. Negatively, we may

not eliminate the evidence that goes contrary to the observation. Positively, the observation recorded in the saying has a counterpart in reality, in the way things happen. But this is not foolproof. The sage, at best, was aware of this.

What claim does a saying like this exert on the modern Bible reader? It presents a biblical insight that has its own circumscribed but valuable point. If modern readers are grappling with the problem of divine retribution, the saying makes a contribution to their understanding, but without exhausting by any means all the aspects of the situation. It is of the utmost importance to evaluate it in the light of its dialectical relationship to other biblical insights on this problem.

Prov 30:18-19

Three things are too wonderful for me;
    four I do not understand:
the way of an eagle in the sky,
    the way of a serpent on a rock,
the way of a ship on the high seas,
    and the way of a man with a maiden.

Context. This saying is grouped along with a number of other so-called numerical sayings (vv 15-16; 21-23; 24-28; 29-31), which have no intrinsic connection with each other except for the numerical formula. The formula consists in giving a number and then exceeding it by one, as a point of emphasis (x and x plus 1). It is an old and established pattern in the ancient New East, and not infrequent in the Bible (cf. Amos 1:3–2:8).

Terms. There is no difficulty with the images that are used, but the repetition of "way" should be noted.

Meaning. The biblical attitude to creation was one of admiration, of wonderment (cf. Psalms 8, 104; Job 38–41). This is also reflected in the saying about the eagle, serpent, ship, and humans. What exactly is the point of the comparisons? One might single out the mystery of movement and ask, How does the eagle succeed in flying, or the serpent (without legs) succeed in moving, or the ship stay afloat and move through the water? Or, one might claim that common to the first three examples is lack of any trace (this indeed seems to be reflected in the metaphors of the ship and bird in Wis 5:10-11). Because of the emphatic repetition of the word, "way," it seems preferable to recognize that the point is *not* that there is no trace left by these movements, but that the trace is not recoverable. One cannot tell where the serpent moved on the rock, nor is there at any point in the air some evidence of how the eagle arrived at where it is, nor how the ship arrived at its position in the sea. When these are seen, they are caught at a given point, as it were. We cannot recover the trajectory they have traveled.

These mysteries culminate in the "way" of a man with a maiden. The point of the saying is to wonder at the particular human situation between a man and a woman: how did it come about, the mystery of its establishment and continuance. The course of the acquaintance is quite irrecoverable. The mystery of sexual attraction and of the life of man and woman together is the object of wonderment.

As we have indicated, the saying is open to more than one interpretation. It is particularly interesting to note Prov 30:20 and see how the saying was applied to a particular situation:

> This is the way of an adulteress:
>> she eats, and wipes her mouth,
>> and says, "I have done no wrong."

Obviously this verse betrays a particular interpretation and application of the numerical saying. Presumably it is a gloss or comment on it. The interpreter singled out the trait that there is no trace left by the objects listed, and then applied this to the supposed reaction of the adulteress. It doesn't matter that the comparison limps more than a little; it was the point which the interpreter chose to emphasize. In doing so, he has restricted the general reach of vv 18-19 and failed to catch its sense of wonderment.

2. Job

Job 1:6-12 (cf. 2:1-10)

Now there was a day when the sons of God came to present themselves before the Lord, and Satan also came among them. The Lord said to Satan, "Whence have you come from?" Satan answered the Lord, "From going to and fro on the earth, and from walking up and down on it." And the Lord said to Satan, "Have you considered my servant Job, that there is none like him on the earth, a blameless and upright man, who fears God and turns away from evil?" Then Satan answered the Lord, "Does Job fear God for nought? Hast thou not put a hedge about him and his house and all that he has, on every side? Thou hast blessed the work of his hands, and his possessions have increased in the land. But put forth thy hand now, and touch all that he has, and he will curse thee to thy face." And the Lord said to Satan, "Behold, all that he has is in your power; only upon himself do not put forth your hand." So Satan went forth from the presence of the Lord.

Context. After the narrative in 1:1-5 has made clear that Job "feared God, and turned away from evil" (1:1), there is a sudden shift in scene to the heavenly court where the Lord reviews the sons of God, among whom is Satan ("adversary"). It is clear from the context that he is not to be identified with the devil or Satan of NT times. He is merely one of the "sons of God" who carry out the Lord's plans. When the Lord asks for agreement from him concerning the integrity of Job, he demurs. He argues that Job serves the Lord only for the material blessings he receives. Then the Lord grants Satan permission to strip Job of his possessions.

Terms. The phrase, "sons of God," designates the members of the heavenly court. They perform various functions for the Lord, such as being his messengers, or "angels." They are explicitly called on in Ps 29:1 to praise the Lord. They are referred to implicitly in Gen 1:26 when the Lord is quoted as taking counsel with them: "Let us make man in our image"; and also in Isa 6:8, when he asks, "Who will go for us?" There is a neat play on words in the text as the Satan asks the Lord, is it "for nought"? (1:9, *ḥinnām*) that Job serves him. The Lord turns this word back on Satan in 2:3 when he accuses Satan of having moved God against him "without cause" (or, "for nought," *ḥinnām*). Both scenes in the heavenly court (1:6-12; 2:1-10) serve to underscore the innocence of Job; he is not suffering for any wrongdoing. Indeed the author explicitly notes that Job did nothing wrong, and he relates Job's resignation to the will of God: "The Lord gave, and the Lord has taken away; blessed be the name of the Lord" (1:21; cf. 2:10).

Meaning. One obvious intention of the passage is to raise the question of the sincerity of Job's service to God. Is he "religious" because of what he gets out of it? Will he be faithful even in adversity? This question is important both in itself for the issue it raises, as well as in its role as a prelude to the dialogue that will ensue.

Nowhere else in the Hebrew Bible is the issue of the quality of one's piety raised as sharply as here. Does religion turn out to be the best guarantee of the good life? And is this the prevailing attitude of humans on earth? Satan's attitude does not necessarily indicate that he is a malevolent power. He simply

refuses to trust human beings on this score. He might be cast in
the role of defender of divine honor: if the Lord knew as much
as Satan did from roaming and patrolling the earth, he would
appreciate his judgment and good intentions. But already a
certain air of hostility appears. Satan pits his own knowledge
against that of the Lord. Moreover, the Lord himself takes up
the *ḥinnām* ("for nought") which Satan used to describe Job's
service in 1:9, to characterize Satan's blind hostility: for nought
you moved me against him. . . . (2:3). Hence Satan is clearly
wrong. His judgment on Job is overturned by the faithful and
generous reaction recorded in 1:21-22 and 2:10.

But other difficulties arise in this context. What kind of God
is this who listens to the doubts raised by one of the "sons of
God"? Is he so uncertain of the sincerity of his creatures that he
accepts the wager laid down by Satan? Even if this scene is
imaginative, and not historical, it suggests an understanding of
the Lord that may seem crude to the modern reader. It may be
that *we* cannot picture the Lord acting in this way, but the
author had no problems about it. First of all, he recognized the
sovereignty of God; Satan can do nothing to Job without divine
approval. In fact the all-pervasive divine causality in the
happenings of this world posed a problem for the Israelite, as
the words of Job (9:22-24) show. God *causes* evil. One solution
to this was to blame the "sons of God" who were invested with
power of judgment in the world and were responsible for
injustice (Psalms 58, 82). In this way the responsibility was
moved a step away from the Lord himself. Israel had no easy
solution to the problem.

One may not infer that the Lord was uncertain about the
loyalty of human creatures. In fact one may make the opposite
inference, namely that he is certain of Job's integrity and
therefore accepts Satan's challenge. One can even argue that he
had to accept it, or he would appear to be fearing for his own

honor, afraid to discover the truth. There would be a nagging fear, if the Lord had turned from the wager.

The function of the prologue (chaps. 1 and 2) is to establish the righteousness of the main character who will be disputing with the friends in the ensuing dialogue. The reader knows something that none of the disputing parties knows! Job is not suffering for wrongdoing, as the friends claim; nor does he himself know the reason. Hence the sympathies of the reader are directed away from the irrelevant, though "orthodox," lectures of the three friends to the reality of Job's integrity. The protagonist has to be an *innocent* sufferer.

Job 3:1-4, 7, 11, 13, 16-17, 20

1 After this Job opened his mouth and cursed the day of his birth.

2 And Job said:

3 "Let the day perish wherein I was born,
    and the night which said,
    'A man-child is conceived.'

4 Let that day be darkness!
    May God above not seek it,
    nor light shine upon it. . . .

7 Yea, let that night be barren;
    let no joyful cry be heard in it. . . .

11 Why did I not die at birth,
    come forth from the womb and expire? . . .

13 For then I should have lain down and been quiet;
    I should have slept; then I should have been at rest, . . .

16 Or why was I not as a hidden untimely birth,
    as infants that never see the light?

17 There the wicked cease from troubling,
    and there the weary are at rest. . . .

20 Why is light given to him that is in misery,
    and life to the bitter in soul?"

Context. Job's complaint leads into the dialogue with his friends. More than a dialogue, chaps. 4–31 constitute a dispute, and they are structured in such a way that Job replies after each one of the three (Eliphaz, Bildad, and Zophar) has spoken. There are three rounds: 4–14, 15–21, and 22–27. The final chapters appear in disarray: Zophar, contrary to the pattern, is given no word, and Job says things that are out of character for him (e.g., 27:13-21). There is no solution to this textual problem, although various redistributions of verses have been proposed by scholars.

Job's opening statement in chap. 3 is a classical example of the biblical "complaint." Normally the laments of the Psalter are lightened by motifs as to why God should intervene and by the certainty that God has heard the prayer of the afflicted psalmist (Psalm 88 is a striking exception). The context of chap. 3 demands that the complaint lack any such motifs. What we read is a bitter curse of the day/night in which Job was born. Time after time during his speeches Job will return to the lamenting posture, but he will also address God in tender terms, appealing to God against God (e.g., 10:3-12). It is a striking fact that the friends address Job alone; Job replies to them, but he also launches out in words to God directly.

Terms. The text above has been shortened for reasons of space and clarity. There are no unusual terms that need explanation, but the reader should note that in the last verses Job is contemplating what life would have been like had he died and gone to Sheol: "There the wicked cease from troubling, and there the weary are at rest" (v 17). Existence in Sheol is seen as a respite from the suffering which afflicts him at present; this motif will occur again in 10:18-19; 14:14.

Meaning. There can be no doubt about the general meaning of the passage. Verse 1 specifies that Job "curses his day," as the Hebrew text puts it literally. His "day" is the time of his birth, as the ensuing lines show, but also his very life or existence. This is developed in the portrayal of day and night as living beings, almost personified. The parallelism of the two time periods serve to structure vv 3-10. He puts the question, Why? that is typical of the biblical lament. However, God is mentioned only indirectly (v 23). In this complaint Job shows a certain restraint which will not appear in the dialogue; there he will direct specific accusations against God. The strophes dealing with "why?" are developed by means of the notion of Sheol, the nonlife in the next world, where all classes of people are given the same treatment. Sheol is the great leveler, and, from Job's point of view, to be preferred to his present existence. He does not raise the problem of his suffering; he merely prefers death. But the strong language is calculated to elicit a response from the three friends who came to console him. What will be their reaction?

● Many devout readers of the Bible are "shocked" by the violent language used by Job (not to mention the language of the psalmists!). Such a reaction is unnecessary. It fails to allow for the fact that Job's reaction is a portrayal that is true to life. By the laws of reality and poetry the author must describe Job as a living and suffering character, and thus complaint is called for. It is significant that utter frankness marks Job's words. Many readers are unwilling to accept their acerbity, even blasphemy. But this is to fail to recognize the familiarity and frankness with which the Israelite addressed the Lord. We may be inhibited by a mistaken concept of God and by an understanding of human endurance that is rather stoic and unbiblical. Indeed, the style of Job's complaint may well serve to correct a starved understanding of humanity and of God.

Job 38:1-7

1 Then the Lord answered Job out of the whirlwind:
2 "Who is this that darkens counsel by words without knowledge?

3. Gird up your loins like a man,
    I will question you, and you shall declare to me.

4 Where were you when I laid the foundations of the
    earth?
    Tell me, if you have understanding.

5 Who determined its measurements—surely you know!
    Or who stretched the line upon it?

6 On what were its bases sunk,
    or who laid its cornerstone,

7 when the morning stars sang together,
    and all the sons of God shouted for joy?"

Context. This is the beginning of the famous "Yahweh speeches" which extend through chaps. 38–41. Job had already expressed a desire for a direct confrontation, sometimes tentatively (13:3; 23:3-7), and sometimes firmly (19:25-27; 31:35-37). One might have expected the theophany immediately after chap. 31, but instead Elihu appears and rattles on in the bombastic style that is characteristic of him. Now the Lord himself finally appears, and the suspense is considerably heightened. What has he to say to his servant?

Terms. The Lord speaks "out of the whirlwind," or storm. Cataclysmic reactions in nature are the usual accompaniment of a theophany in the Bible (cf. Ps 18:7-19; 50:3; Hab 3). Characteristic of the Yahweh speeches are the questions. Instead of formulating an indictment as Job seems to have anticipated in 31:35, the Lord raises a barrage of questions dealing with divine wisdom and power. Job is confronted with, "Do you know?" "Can you?" "Where?" Divine irony is not absent (38:5, 21). Job is given no answer concerning his situation. He is simply led more deeply into divine mystery.

Meaning. The point behind the question in v 4 is the special knowledge that belongs only to one who was present during the act of creation. Of course, Job does not know for he was not present (only personified Wisdom of Prov 8:32 was present, along with the "sons of God"!). Eliphaz had already asked Job if he were as old as the world (15:7-8 and cf. 38:4-7). Since he did not witness creation, his ignorance is the first score against him.

The description of the creation of the world is on the analogy of the construction of a building; the plans for its size (v 5), the setting of the foundations, and the laying of the cornerstone complete the metaphor. Just as a new building is an occasion of celebration (cf. Zech 4:7; Ezra 3:10), so the completion of the creative act becomes a festive scene—for the morning stars and the members of the heavenly court who witness it.

This is not the place to analyze the rest of the speeches. Suffice it to say that they continue in the same mood, questioning Job's knowledge and power over creation. How is this approach of the Lord to be assessed? It is obvious that Job is not given an "answer." Indeed the questions are irrelevant to the life/death situation he is in. Yet they serve three functions. First, they convey the impact of a theophany, the religious experience of a person who is overwhelmed by God's presence. Second, the discourses on creation serve to draw Job (and the reader) ever more deeply into the mystery of God's creation. Third, they succeed in placating, even subduing Job, as 42:5 clearly shows. Job had steadfastly refused to accept the wearisome traditionalism of the three friends. Otherwise he would have denied his own integrity. He had warned them that lies on God's behalf were harmful (13:7-9). His tough-mindedness in his argumentation in the dialogue is obvious; he refused to accept the specious reasoning of his friends. Now when he submits to the Lord he does not go back on his claims, and the Lord admits as much in 42:8, when he tells the friends that they have not spoken rightly of him as Job has. Job does not capitulate to theological argument; he surrenders to God because of a spiritual experience:

> I had heard of thee by the hearing of the ear;
>   but now my eye sees thee. (42:5)

Job submits to the Lord not because he "understands," but because he has had a vision, i.e., an experience of God (which the Yahweh speeches are intended to represent). Job had been of the opinion that God *must* intervene, declare him just, deliver him. If Job has been guilty of anything, it has been his claim that God *must*. Now he has relinquished that claim.

How is the modern reader to interpret these chapters? First of all it is necessary to appreciate the power inherent in the imagery of the various descriptions. Second, they must be seen within the perspective of the entire book. On that level they convey the nature of Yahweh's revelation to Job and his reaction. They do not present an "answer" to him; they spell out the mysterious nature of the Lord, on the basis of which Job can entrust himself to him. Third, the reader is challenged to live with the conviction that suffering is part of the divine mystery, and that it can be endured by those who have an analogous intimate experience of the divine (more than "hearsay," as Job puts it in 42:5).

The high point of the Book of Job comes with his surrender, not with his restoration (42:10-17). The author has put before his readers several points of view to consider. What is the unselfish quality of one's service to God (chaps. 1 and 2)? What is the validity of the traditional theory of retribution (chaps. 3–31)? Should one simply admit that there is no answer for the human condition (chap. 28, wisdom is with God alone)? Also, the restoration of Job simply shows that the author has consistently kept all these options open. God can restore and heal—such is the constant desire expressed in the Psalms—but the divine liberty reigns throughout it all. This is the point so well expressed in "A Masque of Reason" by the poet, Robert Frost, when he portrays God thanking Job for the "demonstration" they put on, in which Job set God free to reign.

3. Ecclesiastes

Eccl 1:2; 12:8

Vanity of vanities, says the Preacher,
  vanity of vanities! All is vanity.
Vanity of vanities, says the Preacher; all is vanity.

Context. Both of these verses are almost the same and occur at key points in the book. Verse 2 really begins the book, since v 1 is merely the superscription. The author, who always speaks in the first person, finishes at 12:8. Since vv 9-14 speak of him in the third person, it is apparently an epilogue added by the editor. Hence we are dealing with a literary *inclusion:* the repetition of an idea at the beginning and end of a unit. The verse is a kind of summary comment (a *Leitmotiv* or motto) on the book, which deals with the author's quest for something that is of substantial and lasting value.

Terms. "Vanity" *(hebel)* is a favorite term of the author, occurring some thirty-seven times in this book. The superlative form, "vanity of vanities" (the utmost vanity), is used only here and in 12:8; both verses are perhaps an editorial expression of the book's message. "Vanity" means literally "breath" or "vapor," hence something insubstantial and ephemeral, of no lasting value.

Because the author generally writes in the first person, and the superlative form occurs only here, this verse may be due to the editor, as mentioned above, but it is a fitting paraphrase of the author's thought. The name the author gives himself in vv 1-12, *qôhelet* (rendered in the RSV as "Preacher") is well nigh untranslatable, and has never been satisfactorily explained. It seems to indicate some relationship to a community or congregation *(qāhāl)*.

Meaning. The statement in itself is an exclamation of utter futility. From the rest of the book, we can see that Qoheleth passes this judgment on all created activity. He consistently characterizes various experiments in living as "vanity": riches, toil, wisdom, and pleasure. There is nothing that he points to as an unmitigated "good" in life, not even "joy" which he frequently (2:26; 3:12, 22; 5:18-19; 8:15; 9:7; 11:8-9) recommends to humans, if God should give it to them. There is no solid "good" for human beings. If they are not thwarted in many concrete ways during life, then the final issue is death, which seals their futility—"How the wise man dies just like the fool!" (2:16). Hence 1:2 and 12:8 sum up the message of the book.

Today it is important to hear well the cry of Qoheleth about the inadequacies of life. His penetrating criticism of the values of his day are a salutary reminder that the myriad of "values" facing the modern person is to be diligently scrutinized. Everyone is called on to pass judgment on true values. Before differing with Qoheleth, we must appreciate his perspective: there is a God, but one cannot make out what God is doing (8:17; 11:5). The honesty of his investigation and his recognition of God's freedom to do what he wants—these are attitudes that surely pertain to the human condition of any age. They are not to be brushed aside by false assurance that virtue yields prosperity.

Eccl 9:1

But all this I laid to heart, examining it all, how the righteous and the wise and their deeds are in the hand of God; whether it is

love or hate man does not know. Everything before them is
vanity.

Context. This is an introduction to a reflection of Qoheleth on
the righteous and the wicked and other classes of people (cf. vv
2-3). He is going to make the point that all have the same lot
(miqreh), that there is no distinction one can make between
them. Life turns out the same for all. The last sentence in v 1 is
textually uncertain, but the RSV adopts a reasonable
emendation.

Terms. Two observations are in order. First, Qoheleth
implicitly identifies the wise with the righteous. This equation,
as we have already seen, runs through the whole wisdom
tradition. Second, one must be clear about the meaning of the
phrase, "hand of God." The Hebrew word, *yād,* means hand,
but is very frequently used in the sense of "power." This
metaphorical use can be seen in a passage such as Job 12:9-10:

> Who among all these does not know
>> that the hand of the Lord has done this?
> In his hand is the life of every living thing
>> and the breath of all mankind.

This verse is rather close to the idea expressed in Eccl 9:1. Job's
emphasis is on the power of God to keep creatures alive, but it is
also clear from the context (Job 12:9; 12:13) that the nuance of
might and all-powerful causality is present (v 14, "if he tears
down, none can rebuild; if he shuts a man in, none can open").
Therefore one should not understand "the hand of God" as
necessarily a caressing, loving hand; in itself it merely indicates
his power. In 9:1, the phrase can be said to be neutral at least; it
designates simply the divine power. But in context the
neutrality turns out to have an edge of hostility. For Qoheleth

says that one cannot tell love from hatred; that is to say, he cannot tell whether God loves him or hates him! The reason is given in vv 2-3: because the same lot (Qoheleth has death primarily in mind; cf. 2:14-15; 3:19-20) is reserved for all. This is repeated more vividly in the several examples that follow in vv 2-3. Here is the heart of his complaint: things turn out the same for all; therefore you cannot tell whether God loves you or hates you.

Meaning. The meaning is clear from the analysis of terms above. Perhaps the modern reader might ask if Qoheleth really intends to say this. There can be no question that this harsh judgment on the human condition is what he meant. At the same time, one must keep his perspective in mind. He is looking at life from the point of view of the sage: what does experience tell us? And he can find nothing here that indicates God's love or hatred. God is simply arbitrary in the way he deals with the good and the evil. The hardest thing to accept is that all have the same lot. One may ask if Qoheleth shared the same faith of his compatriots. Did not the sacred traditions of Israel underscore the goodness and justice of God in the stories of the patriarchs, the Exodus, and the covenant? One may recall Exod 34:6, or the teaching of the prophets about the Lord (e.g., Hos 2:18-23; 11:9). But Qoheleth has bracketed salvation history out of his considerations. He is looking at the fate of human beings from the perspective of the wisdom tradition of observation and experience. Hence we should be careful about drawing any conclusions on the basis of 9:1 as to what Qoheleth might have thought about the saving traditions.

Moreover, we might ask ourselves, How *do* we know that God loves us, or hates us? The answer will be conditioned by our perspective. If the perspective of faith is considered, we may claim that the Lord has revealed this concern, supposedly in Bible and/or tradition. But if one looks at sheer experience and the observation of events in the world, prescinding from the data of one's faith stance, the answer might well be the same as that of Qoheleth: we cannot tell on this basis whether God loves us or hates us.

Finally, the use of the terminology of love/hate when applied to the Divinity may seem strange to us. It is not foreign to the Bible, and we must be careful not to read into this anthropomorphism more than is there. We might translate it into more abstract terms as a divine decision for or against. As Israel read the events of experience, it was clear to her that God either loves or hates.

Eccl 9:10

Whatever your hand finds to do, do it with your might; for there is no work or thought or knowledge or wisdom in Sheol, to which you are going.

Context. This command comes at the end of a recommendation to enjoy whatever pleasures come along in life (wine, white garments, wife, and toil). At several points (2:24; 3:22; 5:18, etc.) Qoheleth urges his readers to partake of whatever joys they can. The verse supplies a command and a motive, to conclude the unit, 9:7-10.

Terms. The meaning of Sheol calls for some comment. In Hebrew thought Sheol, or the nether world, is usually envisioned to be in the belly of the earth, and it is the destination of all who die. It is a kind of nonlife. The body decomposes in the grave, but the Israelites do not speculate on the nature of the one who resides in Sheol (cf. 2 Sam 12:23). Moreover, one has no loving relationship to the Lord (e.g., Ps 6:5). One merely ekes out a kind of shadowy existence.

Meaning. Qoheleth's message is clear: that one should live fully here in this world, because there will be no life ("work or thought") in Sheol after death. Life in the here and now is the only life that the Israelite knew; it means a relationship to the Lord within the covenanted people, which produces blessings for the individual. These are to be enjoyed to the full.

The modern person might well listen to this strong emphasis on living in the here and now. For Qoheleth this is where life is. And that also remains true today; the real problem of living is in the here and now. One can only admire this zest for life, even in the face of all the problems that Qoheleth raises. It is at least better than being in Sheol, or as he puts it in 9:4, "A living dog is better than a dead lion."

However, some might think that this verse has no application to them since they believe in a life with God after death. Thus Christian eschatology, as well as the Jewish belief in the resurrection of the body, provides a perspective that is quite different from that of Qoheleth. One might say that many moderns are on a different time track than that of the Hebrew writer. Can this verse be meaningful to them? Yes, in two ways. First, it centers in on essential value: one should live life to the fullest. For Qoheleth, as for the Israelite, this involved a relationship to the Lord, however mysterious the deity might be. Life is the key term; God is part of it, and the modern would do well to recognize this. Even in a perspective that does not allow for a blessed immortality, life is a treasure to be valued and embraced. In this way one accepts life on God's terms. Second, the agony of Qoheleth is the context for a better appreciation of the gift of eternal life. The "heaven" of popular religion might thus be purified of distortions. It is the gift of God and is rooted in a relationship that is cultivated in this life.

Eccl 12:7

And the dust returns to the earth as it was, and the spirit returns to God who gave it.

Context. This verse comes as a conclusion to Qoheleth's famous poem on old age and death (12:1-6). He can advise the young to rejoice in their youth (11:9). But then he creates a more somber atmosphere: "before the evil days come" (12:1); "before the sun and the light and the moon and the stars are darkened" (12:2); "before the silver cord is snapped" (12:6). In these lines there are certain allegorical traits. Images of the darkness of a storm (v 2), of a desolate homestead (vv 3, 6), and of a dreary old age as the body winds down (vv 3-5) are mixed together to lead into v 7.

Terms. "Dust" is used here to designate the final goal of human life: we return to our origins, the dust from which we were made. This is a reversal of Gen 2:7 which states: "The Lord God formed man of the dust of the ground, and breathed into his nostrils the breath of life; and man became a living being." This understanding of the dependency of life, and thus of human existence, on the breath or spirit of God is typically biblical:

> When thou hidest thy face, they are dismayed;
> > when thou takest away their breath, they die
> > and return to their dust.
> When thou sendest forth thy spirit, they are created;
> > and thou renewest the face of the ground.   (Ps 104:29-30)

In Job 34:14-15 Elihu describes the process in a similar fashion:

> If he [God] should take back his spirit to himself,
> > and gather to himself his breath,
> all flesh would perish together,
> > and man would return to dust.

All things live because of the breathing of God. The return to the dust is a fairly common theme in the Bible (Job 10:9; 34:15).

It underscores the fragility and mortality of human life; in Ps 30:9 dust is personified, as the psalmist asks, "Will the dust praise thee?" In Sheol there will be no praise offered to the Lord.

Several different terms are used for "breath," or "spirit": *rûaḥ* (a common word for wind or spirit) occurs in Eccl 12:7; Ps 104:29-30; *nᵉshāmāh* is the "breath of life" in Gen 2:7. The image is that of breathed-upon matter. When God breathes, there is life; when he takes his breath back (Ps 104:29; Job 34:14), there is no longer any life.

Meaning. This text illustrates the importance of examining the presuppositions that we bring to reading the Bible. Thus, if we start with the assumption that the categories of body and soul are biblical, it is only too easy to find in v 7 a statement of immortality: the body ends in the grave and the soul returns to God. This is contrary to Qoheleth's meaning. Soul and body, as commonly understood, are part of our Greek heritage and are not found in the Hebrew Bible. The analysis of the terms (see above) leads us into the Hebrew world view, which operates with dust and divine breath.

Qoheleth therefore is describing the return of humans to the dust from which they came and the cessation of the divine creative activity represented by the breath of God. We may not infer from this that annihilation or extinction is proposed. There is no speculation among the Israelites about "what" it is that descends to Sheol. It is simply stated that an individual is in Sheol, and there is no attempt to analyze the identity (cf. Eccl 9:10, "in Sheol, to which *you* are going").

This meaning is in harmony with Eccl 3:19-21, where Qoheleth claims that the lot of humans and beasts is the same—it is the same divine breath *(rûaḥ)* that makes them live. Some tried to make a distinction: the human spirit *(rûaḥ)* went upward and the spirit of the beast downward (3:21). Whatever this distinction might amount to, Qoheleth denies it: "Who knows?"

It is clear that 12:7 describes the lot of a human being from the perspective of Israelite belief. Therefore this verse has *nothing* to do with immortality and the return of the "soul" to God. It simply describes the end of human life. Elsewhere in this book (see the remarks on Sir 41:1-4), we point out the challenge that such a perspective presents to anyone who believes in a blessed immortality.

4. The Song of Songs (Canticles)

Properly speaking, this work is made up of love poems, rather than sayings and admonitions that are characteristic of Wisdom Literature. However, several modern scholars are inclined to believe that the sages may have been responsible for the preservation and transmission of these eight chapters, published under the title, "The Song of Songs by Solomon." The repetition of the word "song" reflects the Hebrew means of expressing the superlative: the best or greatest song (cf. "king of kings," "lord of lords"). That authorship is attributed to Solomon perhaps suggests a wisdom influence in the assembling of these poems, and Solomon's reputation as the possessor of a large harem (1 Kgs 11:3) could have served to suggest him as a qualified author.

Scholarship has not been able to offer any sure conclusions about the composition of the Song. Are these disparate poems that have been welded together? How many are there? Is the Song really a drama (with two main characters, Solomon and a young woman, or possibly three, if her peasant lover is included)? For practical purposes, it is suggested that the reader approach the Song as essentially a dialogue between a man and a woman. Many translations (NEB, NAB) provide identification rubrics for the speakers, and fortunately these may be regarded as certain for over 90 percent of the text.

● In chapter 2 a brief sketch of the history of the Song of Songs was provided, and the role of the assumptions which readers have brought to this book was underlined. Two important assumptions for the interpretation of the Songs are adopted here: (1) these are love poems which reflect the yearning and experience of love between a man and a woman; (2) the songs were collected and edited and eventually found their way into the Hebrew canon, perhaps because they were seen to contribute to the stability of human life, and/or perhaps because they were understood as a kind of parable concerning the covenant relationship between the Lord and his people.

Song of Songs 2:8-17

8   The voice of my beloved!
        Behold, he comes,
      leaping upon the mountains,
        bounding over the hills.
9   My beloved is like a gazelle,
        or a young stag.
      Behold, there he stands
        behind our wall,
      gazing in at the windows,
        looking through the lattice.
10 My beloved speaks and says to me:
      "Arise, my love, my fair one,
        and come away;
11 for lo, the winter is past,
        the rain is over and gone.
12 The flowers appear on the earth,
        the time of singing has come,
      and the voice of the turtledove
        is heard in our land.

13 The fig tree puts forth its figs,
    and the vines are in blossom;
    they give forth fragrance.
Arise, my love, my fair one,
    and come away.

14 O my dove, in the clefts of the rock,
    in the covert of the cliff,
let me see your face,
    let me hear your voice,
for your voice is sweet,
    and your face is comely.

15 Catch us the foxes,
    the little foxes,
that spoil the vineyards,
    for our vineyards are in blossom."

16 My beloved is mine and I am his,
    he pastures his flock among the lilies.

17 Until the day breathes
    and the shadows flee,
turn, my beloved, be like a gazelle,
    or a young stag upon rugged mountains.

Context. This unit can be separated from the previous verses which featured a dialogue between the man and the woman, because now she speaks in order to recall a visit paid to her by the man. The narrative seems to continue to the end of the chapter, since 3:1 introduces a new episode in which she relates his absence and the search for him. The careful reader will note the *inclusion* which occurs between vv 8-9 and 17 (the repetition of "gazelle," "stag," "mountains"), and especially between vv 10 and 13 ("arise, my love . . ."). The woman speaks in vv 9-13; the man speaks in v 14; and she replies in v 15 and continues in vv 16-17.

Terms. There are no unusual terms, but the use of many

poetic images is somewhat novel. This is characteristic of the language and imagery of the Song. There is a profusion of fruits and flowers: vineyard, henna, cedars and cypresses, figs and pomegranates, myrrh and aloes, palms, herbs, and mandrakes. Many types of animals appear: stags, gazelles, hinds and fawns, doves, and foxes. The unit opens with a vivid description of the man's eagerness to be with his beloved and the invitation to a tryst which he issues to her. The association of spring and the awakening of love is a perennial theme in love literature. In v 14 he addresses her as a "dove in the clefts of the rock" and asks to see and hear her. She replies with an enigmatic verse (15) about the "little foxes." She answers his request to hear her voice, but one cannot be sure of her meaning. It may be a tease, reminding him that little foxes (other men) go after the vineyards (a symbol for women) when they are in bloom. Hence the lover would do well to attend to the woman who might be besieged by other suitors. Verse 16 appears to be a refrain (cf. 6:3; 7:10) about their mutual love, and the woman ends the unit with an invitation that reaches back to the symbolism of vv 8-9. As the footnote to the RSV translation indicates, "rugged" is an uncertain rendering of the Hebrew text.

Meaning. Love poetry utilizes many themes; it expresses yearning, joy, affection, praise of beauty, mutual teasing, presence/absence of the beloved, fidelity, and other attitudes. All these are unified by the dominant desire of love and mutual possession. The beauty of the poetry lies in the skill and imagination by which these emotions are expressed. The woman succeeds in a vivid re-creation of the visit and invitation from her lover which is more than just factual. It conveys the intensity of the love that exists between them. By taking up the symbols of vv 8-9 in her final words she has replied to his invitation; she invites him to herself.

● It may be argued that love poems only have meaning for the lovers concerned, the poet and the beloved. But they also serve to inspire those who read them, as history shows. The fact that they have been collected and form part of the Bible is a sign to the Believing Community that sexuality is essentially a good thing. The first chapters of Genesis have already said this in a matter of fact sort of way. But now love between the sexes is celebrated in the Song, and the simple episode in 2:8-17 illustrates how memory, mood, desire, and nature itself can come together to express the reality of love. The language of love is not easy to learn, and it can become tired, as love itself. Here the Song serves as a model. It has the power of awakening in the reader unsuspected depths of feeling for the beloved. This passage questions us with regard to the expression of love in our own lives. While it has a direct bearing on human sexual love, it can also serve in a transferred meaning to illuminate other experiences of human love (see the history of interpretation of the Song in chapter 2).

Song of Songs 8:6

Set me as a seal upon your heart,
    as a seal upon your arm;
for love is strong as death,
    jealousy is cruel as the grave.
Its flashes are flashes of fire,
    a most vehement flame.

Context. The Hebrew text indicates that these lines are spoken by the woman to the man. The Song is made up of dialogue between these two characters, who admire and take joy in each other. The previous verse (5) is spoken by the man, according to the Hebrew vocalization, and v 7 continues the woman's exalted description of love.

Terms. The "seal" could be worn around the neck (Gen 38:18) and thus on the "heart," or also on the hand as a ring (Jer 22:24). It could serve as identification (Gen 38:18) or signature purposes. The point of the woman's request is the inseparability of lover and beloved. The comparison of love to death hinges on the meaning of "death." Death is frequently personified in OT thought as a power, and here it is parallel to the "grave," or Sheol (cf. Pss 18:5; 49:14; 89:48). Death or Sheol pursues every human being to the end, and the lover's pursuit of the beloved is thus comparable to this dynamic understanding of death. The term "jealousy" is simply parallel to the word, "love," and it indicates "ardor," and does not have the suggestion of an uncertain and selfish love. Similarly, "cruel" is better rendered by "unyielding," or "intense."

"Flashes of fire" indicates another aspect of the power of love: its intensity is metaphorically expressed by comparison with fire. "A most vehement flame" is a possible translation of the Hebrew word, but it could also be rendered as "a flame of Yah (Yahweh)." If so translated, this would be the only reference to God in the entire work.

Meaning. The request of the woman is in line with the desires that she expresses throughout the work. But such a desire does not need a motivation, contrary to the RSV translation, "for." It would be better to understand this as an exclamation about the nature of love between man and woman ("indeed," and leave "for" out of the text). Such love is as strong as any power known in human experience, such as Death/Sheol. The intensity of love is further suggested by the comparison to fire. If the translation, "a flame of Yah (Yahweh)," suggested above, is accepted, another theme is added: the fire of love is not without a relationship to the Lord—but that relationship is not specified.

The desire for intimacy and the power of love are surely not unknown to the modern person. What is important is that the Bible underscores it in a positive way, and if the above translation is accepted, correlates it with the love of the Lord. Earlier in the work (7:10), the woman remarked that the man's "yearning" was for her, thus deliberately reversing the statement in Gen 3:16 that the woman's yearning was for the man. Love is seen in the Song as mutual and powerful and is obviously affirmed as good. Somewhat mysteriously, it seems to be associated with the Lord ("flame of Yah").

● Does this verse have a meaning over and beyond sexual love between a man and a woman? There is nothing in the text to suggest that this was the intention of the writer. Nonetheless, the fact remains that the Song has been consistently interpreted by both synagogue and church as referring to the love of God and his people. Specific variations on this theme (Christ and the church: God and the individual soul) occur in Christian tradition. Is this a misreading or does it have some validity even if it goes beyond the literal historical meaning of the text? First, it should be noted that the symbolism of sexual love between husband and wife is a recurrent theme in the Prophets, especially in Hosea 1–3. Israel herself seized on this peak human experience to convey the depths of the covenant relationship between the Lord and his people. Second, one may ask if love is not essentially a participatory thing: love in God and in humans is an analogous, not a univocal concept. The experiences common to the different levels, human and divine, are the same: presence and absence, yearning for the beloved, praise of and joy in the beloved. The sexual relationship reflects a divine reality ("a flame of Yahweh"), and hence one learns both that human love is a participation in divine love, and that divine love can be described and understood in the passionate songs of the Canticle.

5. Ecclesiasticus (Sirach)

Sir 41:1-4

1 O death, how bitter is the reminder of you
    to one who lives at peace among his possessions,
  to a man without distractions, who is prosperous in everything,
    and who still has the vigor to enjoy his food!
2 O death, how welcome is your sentence
    to one who is in need and is failing in strength,
  very old and distracted over everything;
    to one who is contrary, and has lost his patience!
3 Do not fear the sentence of death;
    remember your former days and the end of life;
  this is the decree from the Lord for all flesh,
4   and how can you reject the good pleasure of the Most High?
  Whether life is for ten or a hundred or a thousand years,
    there is no enquiry about it in Hades.

The volumes of the series, Interpreting Biblical Texts, usually restrict themselves to the books of the Hebrew Bible, which correspond to the canon of Protestant Christianity. However, both the Roman Catholic and the Greek (Orthodox) tradition have worked with a larger canon in which seven of the so-called apocryphal books are included—Tobit, Judith, 1 and 2 Maccabees, Baruch, Ecclesiasticus, and Wisdom. Since two important wisdom books (Sirach, Wisdom of Solomon) are included, it is proper that we examine a few passages from them. These books may be read in the spirit of John Bunyan who gives a touching testimony to an experience he had with Sir 2:10:

For thus it was expounded to me: Begin at the beginning of Genesis, and read to the end of Revelation, and see if you can find, that there was any that ever trusted in the Lord, and was

confounded. So, coming home I presently went to my Bible to
see if I could find that saying, not doubting but to find it
presently, . . . Well, I looked but I found it not. . . . Thus I
continued above a year, and could not find the place; but at last,
casting my eye into the Apocrypha books, I found it in
Ecclesiasticus [2:10]. This, at the first, did somewhat daunt me;
but because, by this time, I had got more experience of the love
and kindness of God, it troubled me the less; especially when I
considered that though it was not in those Texts that we call Holy
and Canonical, yet forasmuch as this sentence was the sum and
substance of many of the Promises, it was my duty to take the
comfort of it; and I bless God for that word, for it was of God to
me: that word doth still, at times, shine before my face.[2]

Context. This is a fairly straightforward text which opens a
new topic in this book. Ben Sira contrasts two human attitudes
toward death. For some it is a tragedy, for others it is a blessing.
All depends on the quality of life that one is experiencing. He
merely registers the attitudes in vv 1-2, and this leads him
directly into advice in vv 3-4: accept death with resignation. It is
a simple ineluctable fact. It is to be accepted with equanimity
because it has been decreed by God, and because Sheol
("Hades" is the Greek word for Sheol) has the final word, no
matter how long one lives.

The finality of Sheol/Death is reflected in other parts of this
work (e.g., 38:16-23), as well as in the entire Hebrew Bible (cf.,
e.g., Ps 49:7-11). There existed a remarkable attitude of
resignation in the face of death. Ben Sira (Sirach) shared in this
understanding, but in 41:1-4 he is imaginative and realist
enough to contrast differing attitudes, even while he comes
down on the side of the divine decree, the universality, and
inevitability of death.

[2]*Grace Abounding* (John Brown edition, 1888), 63-65.

Terms. The sense of "distract" in vv 1-2 is that of annoyances or problems. The Hebrew original of v 3 would suggest that "former days and the end of life" should be understood in the sense of "all those before you and after you."

Meaning. This text contains an observation and a recommendation. It witnesses to the Israelite attitude to Death/Sheol and its finality. In this respect it reflects the simple acceptance of the dimensions of life established by the Lord. It does not deny that the divine decree can be received with mixed feelings, depending on the quality of life experienced by a human being. But the author cuts through this with a firm command: Fear not, accept the situation!

This text might appear, at first sight, to have little to say to those who believe in a meaningful afterlife (i.e., those who believe in a "heaven," however that might be defined, and who do not have "Sheol" in their working vocabulary). Sirach's text puts a question to the reader who is operating in such a framework, Does a personal belief in a blessed afterlife tempt one to take death less seriously? If one believes, for example, with Saint Paul, that death has lost its "sting" (1 Cor 15:54-57), does this create a sense of unreality about death? Is it possible that a belief in a future existence can distort human perspectives on God and religion? Many Christians who are future oriented by reason of their eschatological beliefs profess to be astounded at the absence of such a belief in the Hebrew Bible. (It is only with the Book of Daniel that a doctrine of a future life is seen clearly to emerge; cf. Dan 12:2.) The astonishment of some modern readers is so great that they are prompted to say, "Then how could the Israelite believe in God?" Such a perverted reaction shows the need for a text like Sir 41:1-5. So central has a belief in a future life become to such an individual that it has been confused with faith in God. It is as if faith could be based only on the existence of life with God after death. Such a distortion is destructive of the very notion of faith. It is Sirach who has faith in God; he accepts God on God's terms; he has his priorities straight. It is up to God to reveal the reality of a blessed immortality beyond death. Since God had given no indication of this, Sirach's faith is clear and admirable. The faith of the person who does accept a revelation of "heaven" may find a much needed purification by contemplating the stalwart faith of this second-century Jew.

Sir 24:1-23

1 Wisdom will praise herself,
   and will glorify herself in the midst of the people.
2 In the assembly of the Most High she will open her mouth,
   and in the presence of his host she will glory;
3 "I came forth from the mouth of the Most High,
   and covered the earth like a mist.
4 I dwelt in high places,
   and my throne was in a pillar of cloud.
5 Alone I have made the circuit of the vault of heaven,
   and have walked in the depths of the abyss.
6 In the waves of the sea, in the whole earth,
   and in every people and nation I have gotten a possession.
7 Among all these I sought a resting place;
   I sought in whose territory I might lodge.

8 Then the Creator of all things gave me a commandment,
   and the one who created me assigned a place for my tent.
   And he said, 'Make your dwelling in Jacob,
   and in Israel receive your inheritance.'
9 From eternity, in the beginning, he created me,
   and for eternity I shall not cease to exist.
10 In the holy tabernacle I ministered before him,
   and so I was established in Zion.
11 In the beloved city likewise he gave me a resting place,
   and in Jerusalem was my dominion.

12   So I took root in an honored people,
       in the portion of the Lord, who is their inheritance.

13   I grew tall like a cedar in Lebanon, ..."

(In vv 14-17 Wisdom continues such metaphors, "like a palm tree," and then closes her speech in vv 19-22.)

19   "Come to me, you who desire me,
       and eat your fill of my produce.
20   For the remembrance of me is sweeter than honey,
       and my inheritance sweeter than the honeycomb.
21   Those who eat me will hunger for more,
       and those who drink me will thirst for more.
22   Whoever obeys me will not be put to shame,
       and those who work with my help will not sin."

23   All this is the book of the covenant of the Most High God,
       the law which Moses commanded us
       as an inheritance for the congregations of Jacob.

Context. See the comments on Proverbs 8 above for the personification of Wisdom, and the broader context. Sirach 24 is a reinterpretation of Proverbs 8.

Terms. A brief summary of the movement of thought can suffice here. Lady Wisdom speaks about herself, but this time it is in the heavenly court (v 2), and not in the crowded squares of the city (Prov 8:2-3). She once more proclaims her divine origin, and the emphasis is on her preexistence. Her participation in creation (Proverbs 8) is not mentioned. Instead she describes an existence in the heavens with the Lord where she has free run of creation ("vault of heaven," "depths of the abyss," "waves of the sea"). She seems to be in a perpetual round of activity, seeking a place where she might dwell. Finally the Creator commands her: Settle in Jacob! She does so, and she describes how she offers worship (*eleitourgēsa,* liturgical worship) to the Lord in the Jerusalem temple (v 10). Then she describes herself as a tree, a vine, a garden of exotic plants whose branches and blossoms are glorious and rich (vv 13-18). She invites those who desire her to eat and drink of her rich fruits. Paradoxically, their hunger and thirst will only be increased, yet steadily replenished.

Meaning. The above paraphrase brings out the meaning adequately. Wisdom is personified as a heavenly, eternal, and cosmic figure, originating from God. She seeks a dwelling place on earth and obeys the divine command to dwell in Jerusalem, where she promises sustenance to those who partake of her. In contrast to Proverbs 8, there is great emphasis on Wisdom's journey from the heavens to the earth. The important move of Ben Sira is in v 23 were he explicitly identifies Wisdom with the Torah, or Law. For him Wisdom has become the particular revelation of the divine will in the Mosaic Law. This point of view is expressed also in Deut 4:6-8, where Moses urges the Israelites to fidelity to the "statutes and ordinances":

> "Keep them and do them; for that will be your wisdom and your understanding in the sight of the peoples, who, when they hear all these statutes, will say, 'Surely this great nation is a wise and understanding people.' For what great nation is there that has a god so near to it as the Lord our God is to us, whenever we call upon him? And what great nation is there, that has statutes and ordinances so righteous as all this law which I set before you this day?"

Many of the sayings in Sirach reflect this identification of Wisdom and Law (e.g., 15:1; 21:11, etc.).

● This passage from Sirach illustrates a valuable insight; The biblical tradition moves; it does not stand still. Wisdom means one thing in Proverbs, but by the second century B.C., it has been swept into the Torah ("Law"), transfiguring what might appear to some as merely picayune points of legal observance. Now the discernment of and devotion to God's will is seen in a new light. This move challenges the modern reader to reassess his or her understanding of Israel's Law. There is more than one point of view (e.g., that of Saint Paul) available in the Bible.

6. Wisdom of Solomon

Wis 1:14-15

14 For he created all things that they might exist,
        and the creatures of the world are wholesome,
    and there is no destructive poison in them;
        and the dominion of Hades is not on earth.
15 For righteousness is immortal.

Context. This stunning claim occurs in a context in which the author is opposing God to death (Wis 1:12-16). He warns his readers that wickedness leads to death (1:12) and proclaims that death is not part of the divine plan (1:13). But as one continues to read this passage, it appears that the writer has more than just physical death in mind. He means both physical and spiritual death (alienation from God). He develops the idea that the whole purpose of God's creation-act is life, not death. All things created by him are "wholesome" (cf. the "goodness" of creation in Gen 1). Moreover Sheol (the Greek word is *Hadēs*) no longer has dominion over all creatures. Rather, it is the wicked who belong to death. They are described as having "made a covenant" with death (1:16), so closely are their persons and deeds identified with it. Indeed, it appears that death is associated only with the wicked, whereas life belongs to the wise, or the righteous. This view underlies the statement in 1:15.

Terms. The word translated by "immortal" is *athanatos,* i.e., it is the Greek word for "death" *(thanatos),* preceded by what is called the "privative" *a.* Thus the word denotes the negation of death: non-death or undying.

"Righteousness" is *dikaiosynē,* a key word in Pauline theology. What does it mean here? How is one to conceive of OT righteousness? One might take a cue from Abraham, who believed in God, and "he reckoned it to him as righteousness" (Gen 15:6). It was Abraham's relationship to the Lord, one of faith and love as Genesis 12–22 shows, that constituted his righteousness. Hence righteousness is relational; it designates a vital relationship with the Lord. One might say that Psalm 73 presents a description of such a relationship:

> 23 Nevertheless I am continually with thee;
>   thou dost hold my right hand. . . .
> 26 My flesh and my heart may fail,
>   but God is the strength of my heart and my portion for ever.
>   (Ps 73:23, 26)

Meaning. Verse 15 makes a remarkable claim: between God and humans there exists an undying relationship. Humans can exit from this relationship, but it is nonetheless offered to them. Israel had long known that it was the Lord who "brings down to Sheol and raises up" (1 Sam 2:6). He was surely stronger than death, and the psalmists acknowledge this (Pss 33:19; 56:13). What is new here is that death does not sever this relationship. It can go on, as far as humans are concerned; they may give it up or set it aside by transgression (as do the "impious" described in Wisdom 2). But *from God's side* the relationship perdures; it is undying.

This statement about human immortality is one of several in

the book (e.g., see 2:23; 3:1-3). What is truly remarkable is the *manner* in which immortality is conceived. The writer does not argue for immortality on the basis of an intrinsic human nature, i.e., that the human soul is of such a nature that it never dies, or that the human body, even though it corrupts, will rise again. The writer says nothing about these two possibilities even if he may have accepted them. Both of those views deal with the *manner* of immortality in terms of the composition of the human being. This is *not* what the writer is talking about. It is possible that the Greek idea of the immortality of the soul acted as a catalyst in his thought, but he understands immortality on a more basic level. It has to do with one's relationship to God—this is the *positive* meaning of immortality. It is not merely an extension in time by means of a spiritual soul or a risen body. It is a relationship between the righteous and the Lord which will of itself never die. Humans alone can sever it, and so lose immortality as it is understood in the rich sense that the author attaches to it. He is really not interested in immortality conceived of as merely continuation in time beyond physical death. There is no curiosity expressed about the fate of those who lack righteousness and therefore by definition do not belong to "the immortals." They are said to "suffer anguish" (4:19) and the anguish of the impious is described in 5:1-8. But they are not said to be immortal; they lack that essential relationship to God.

What does this text mean to the modern reader? It is particularly relevant to one who claims to believe in immortality, in "heaven," or in whatever else a blessed afterlife might be expressed. And this is so because it puts the question squarely, What does immortality mean? Is it a question of living forever, or does it have to do more with the quality of life—living with God? Whereas much of popular religion emphasizes reward and punishment (heaven and hell), the Book of Wisdom calls one back to essentials: the meaning of life with God and the continuity of a relationship which death cannot interrupt although we can choose to ignore or even destroy that relationship.

IV. ISRAEL'S PRAYER—THE PSALMS

The word "psalm" derives from the Greek *psalmos,* meaning the music associated with a stringed instrument. The word came to be applied to the song which the music accompanied. Eventually Jewish tradition gave the name *tehillim* (songs of praise) to the final collection. The Psalms number one hundred fifty, and they are drawn from various historical periods, before and after the Exile. It appears that several collections came to be formed, and a fivefold division within the Psalter is indicated by the doxologies which appear at the end of Psalms 41, 78, 89, and 106.

1. Presuppositions

As with the wisdom books (chaps. 1 and 2), we now consider presuppositions concerning the interpretation of the Psalms. Again, there is no intention of prescribing for the reader, to whom any decision must be left; nonetheless, certain assumptions will be seen as more profitable than others.

1. The titles (superscriptions) of the various psalms are at least as old as the so-called Septuagint translation of the Hebrew Bible into Greek about 200 B.C. They witness to a

venerable Jewish tradition about authorship, about liturgical and musical instructions, and often about the historical setting in which a psalm was supposedly written. Current biblical scholarship regards the data about authorship (some seventy-five psalms are attributed to David) and setting (e.g., Psalm 51, "when Nathan the prophet came to him [David], after he had gone in to Bathsheba") as overprecise. We have no real evidence about what psalms, if any, David wrote. Similarly, the original setting of the various prayers escapes us. The suggestions of modern biblical scholarship are more modest than the claims laid down in the superscriptions to the Psalms. The setting is only vaguely, if wisely, suggested by the literary classification of songs of praise, thanksgiving, lament (individual and community), and other types.

It is natural enough, if one believes that David is the author of a given psalm, to attempt to assign it to a certain point in his career as presented in 1 and 2 Samuel and in 2 Chronicles. But this means stacking one hypothesis upon another. Moreover, this approach particularizes and historicizes a prayer that originally had a broader usage than the life of this king. Some may find a solution to the alleged Davidic authorship by claiming that the attribution leads one to see in David an Everyman, or universal figure with whom one can identify.[1] Others may find that such ascription to David (or to Moses, Psalm 90, or to Solomon, Psalm 72) is too restrictive and crippling. In any case, this tradition about authorship is simply unverifiable.

2. Most of the Psalms were composed in the first instance for liturgical celebration. They are not just Hebrew poems—by David or some other individual—that came to be used at some time in the liturgy; they were composed for such a purpose.

[1]Cf. B. Childs, *Introduction to the Old Testament as Scripture* (Philadelphia: Fortress Press, 1979), pp. 520-22.

Often one can discern the role of the psalmist as a master of ceremonies as he gives orders to the community relative to their participation in the celebration (e.g., Ps 118:1-4). There are innumerable references to the temple itself and to liturgical celebrations which enable the careful reader to enter into the spirit of Israel's liturgy.

Again, it seems wise to abstain from extreme hypothesizing. For example, was there an annual feast of the Enthronement of Yahweh in which psalms like 93, 96–100 would have played a role? This theory, elaborated in great detail by S. Mowinckel *(The Psalms in Israel's Worship,* Abingdon, 1962) may not convince everyone, but it does open up to the reader insights into Israel's liturgy and theology.

3. The so-called messianic psalms deal with the currently reigning king: a royal wedding (Psalm 45), accession to the throne or its anniversary (Psalm 72), attitude before and after a battle (Psalms 20, 21). The word Messiah means "anointed," and the anointed one *par excellence* was the king, not the high priest whose role was more prominent in the postexilic period when there was no king.

It is difficult for us to appreciate the central role of the king in the ancient Near East. He was divinized in Egypt, and nearly so in Mesopotamia. In Israel the prophets spoke out against kings, but the monarch was still a sacral figure, the channel through whom divine blessings were to come to the people. In Judah the unconditional divine promise issued to David (2 Samuel 7) became the mainstay of his dynasty. This promise was developed in the prophetic writings (esp. in Isaiah 7–12, "the book of Immanuel"), and it was the basis of the messianic hope for a future king "like David," who would reign in Jerusalem.

While the royal or "messianic" psalms refer therefore to each currently reigning king, they nevertheless entered the Hebrew Canon in the postexilic period when there was no longer any kingship in Jerusalem. Why were they preserved? Because they were reinterpreted in the light of the divine promise: there would be another like David! In a similar way Christian tradition (cf. Luke 1:32-33, and the Christian liturgies) reinterpreted these royal psalms as referring to Jesus Christ. But obviously they are not predictions, since they refer historically to the reigning king.

● 4. The prayers in the OT are by no means all found in the Psalter (cf. Moses in Num 11:11-15; Abraham in Gen 18:23-33; David in 2 Sam 7:18-29), but the Psalms form the heart of Israel's prayer. In fact they are a "school of prayer" in the sense that they teach one how to pray. Prayer need not be vocal, but most often it is put into words. And what is one to say? How does one pray? The Psalms answer this question by their variety, their vividness, and their boldness.

First, the variety of the Psalms conveys the entire range of human emotions before God: praise, thanksgiving, complaint, resignation, joy, anguish, trust, and awe. Prayer is not simply asking for things: it is the varied expression of the human condition in the presence of God. And it is precisely this variety of ways in which a human being can address God that is illustrated in the Psalter.

Second, there is the vividness of the imagery. A great deal of biblical symbolism has entered into our modern and Western heritage, but we are hardly prepared for phrases like "horn of salvation," or the "bulls of Bashan" or "mountains that skip like rams." The modern reader, in becoming more conversant with the world view of the Bible, will slowly absorb the imagery that characterizes it. When the author of Psalms 69 speaks of sinking "in deep mire, where there is no foothold," or when we hear "out of the depths I cry to thee" (130:1), we catch these metaphors almost at once. We, too, have been there—in distress and abandonment. In such language the biblical writer is using the metaphor of Sheol (the realm of the dead; see the exegesis of Sirach 41 in chapter 3) to convey a distressful human situation. This symbol of Sheol suits modern needs as well.

Third there is the boldness of the language used in the Psalter. The Lord will be curtly told to awake from sleep (Ps 44:23) and to intervene in favor of a suffering people. God is challenged to judge the psalmist according to his integrity (26:1, 11). The question Why? is hurled at the deity several times (22:1; 74:1). The familiarity with which Israel addressed the Lord may prove disconcerting to some modern tastes. But when one looks carefully at the faith and trust from which it springs, it becomes not only more intelligible, but even "proper."

However, many readers draw the line at the violence and vengeance especially manifested against "enemies," which come to expression in the Psalms. This seems to be a more difficult obstacle to hurdle. One may object that "prayer" is the time and place for forgiveness and not for vengeful feelings. Such reactions, while justifiable in themselves, are off the mark. One does not pray simply in order to cultivate "pious thoughts," or in order to enter an unreal world that is not shadowed by human sinfulness. Prayer is best geared to reality, which is imperfect and sinful. Three considerations may be of help to people who feel uneasy about such passages as Pss 109; 137:7-9; 139:19-22. First, the perspective of the psalmist has to be understood. The extravagant imprecations are an indication of how seriously Israel believed in divine justice. (It remains true that human standards of justice are often in conflict with the mystery of God.) Divine justice should be manifested in this life, which was the only life that Israel knew. Hence the imprecations against evildoers: let God's justice be done. Such a perspective has to be understood, rather than condemned in an offhand way. Second, the language is deliberately exaggerated. The conflict between good and evil, between righteousness and wickedness, is expressed in cosmic terms. The spirit is opposed by the flesh, the divine by the human; a maximum godlessness is incarnated in the wicked. This makes for extravagance in the expression of judgment and feelings. Finally, it may remain true that a modern reader simply prefers not to voice such vengeance and violence. Basically, the discomfort comes from the way in which the psalm is appropriated. Usually one identifies with the psalmist, and when the psalm is expressing praise and confidence this approach is successful. But it is not the only approach. In the case of the so-called cursing psalms one can and should *hear* the agony of the psalmist. This is not a passive listening but an active reading. The cry of the psalmist then serves to make us aware of the violence and vengeance that lurk in our own hearts, the violence that characterizes the society in which we live and for which we bear some responsibility. Then such passages can be a mirror of our own spiritual condition, an accusation against our own violence or complacency toward violence. Instead of judging the psalmist we judge ourselves; this is more profitable then eliminating such passages (as is done in certain aseptic "prayer" books), or simply skipping them.

5. Because these prayers are written over a period of some seven centuries they constitute a profile of biblical theology. They will accordingly be the more easily appreciated in proportion to the understanding and appreciation of the faith of the Israelite community. Much insight on this score can be had from such books as H. Ringgren, *The Faith of the Psalmists* (Fortress Press, 1963) and from G. von Rad, *Old Testament Theology* (Harper & Row, 1962) I, 356-408.

• The psalmist had a flair for recreating the events of salvation history, such as the deliverance at the Exodus, or the giving of the Torah, so that these events are represented (cf. Deut 5:1-3) in the liturgical celebration. The challenge to the modern reader is the measure to which he or she can recognize their spiritual roots in Israel's traditions. When Zion or Jerusalem is the object of wonderment and praise, this is not just a matter of ancient history, or geographical location. Zion connotes the presence of the Lord among the people, and this forms the heart of such prayers as Psalms 46, 48 (see the treatment of Psalm 48 below). It is imperative to enter into the understanding and spirit of such psalms. (On "presence" in the Psalms, see R. E. Murphy, "The Faith of the Psalmist," *Interpretation* 34 [1980] 229-39.)

2. Selections from Psalms

The Torah: Psalm 1

1 Blessed is the man
      who walks not in the counsel of the wicked,
   nor stands in the way of sinners,
      nor sits in the seat of scoffers;
2 but his delight is in the law of the Lord,
      and on his law he meditates day and night.
3 He is like a tree
      planted by streams of water,
   that yields its fruit in its season,
      and its leaf does not wither.
   In all that he does, he prospers.

4 The wicked are not so,
      but are like chaff which the wind drives away.
5 Therefore the wicked will not stand in the judgment,
      nor sinners in the congregation of the righteous;
6 for the Lord knows the way of the righteous,
      but the way of the wicked will perish.

The Psalter opens with a psalm that is not so much a prayer as a description of two classes of people, the just and the wicked. It pronounces a blessing on the righteous and contrasts their fate with that of the wicked.

Structure. Here one finds a straightforward comparison between the righteous and the wicked, in two strophes (vv 1-3, 4-6). There is probably some significance to the fact that such a theme was chosen to introduce the entire collection. Thereby, a didactic purpose is at work; the Psalms are assembled under the banner of righteousness and wickedness, and the reader is called on to make a choice (cf. Deut 30:15-20).

Terms. Characteristic of this psalm is the emphasis on the Law, or Torah, which is the constant preoccupation, indeed, the joy of the righteous. From this flows prosperity. The attitude of the wicked to the Law is presumed rather than described; the metaphors of chaff and judgment are applicable here. Probably the judgment of the community is meant in v 5, since its parallel is the assembly or "congregation of the righteous." This might have been interpreted later as the eschatological judgment, but the word itself is general in meaning.

Meaning. At first sight it may be disconcerting to see this particular psalm as the opening composition. It is really not a prayer in the sense of the many types to be found in the one hundred and fifty Psalms, such as songs of praise, thanksgiving, laments, liturgies. Psalm 1 is rather a blessing or a "beatitude," pronounced on those who observe the Torah. This "legal" piety is reflected also in Ps 19:7-13, and especially in Psalm 119, each verse of which carries a reference to the Law (such as: statutes, ordinance, word). Its position at the beginning of the Psalter adds another dimension to Israel's liturgical prayers: it suggests that these compositions teach us about priorities, particularly the will of God as revealed in the Torah. On this level the psalm constitutes a powerful motivation for the Israelite to ascertain the divine will, and this is no mean achievement.

• The presuppositions of a Christian may be an obstacle to the appreciation and appropriation of this ideal. It might be held, for example, that such an emphasis on Law is contrary to the spirit of the NT (see Galatians and Romans). But one should examine carefully the point of conflict in these Epistles. The situation is polemical; Paul is correcting the attitude of Christians who attribute saving power to human works (the Torah), as opposed to saving faith in Christ. This first-century problem need not be the existential situation of a modern Christian who is struggling to carry out the will of God. One can still uphold the saving power of faith in Christ without denigrating good works, since these flow from the spirit of God. There is a certain dialectic within the NT concerning "faith and works": "So faith by itself, if it has no works, is dead" (James 2:17).

Hence one may approach Psalm 1 in the spirit of both/and, instead of either/or. Works proclaim faith. Of course, Psalm 1 may not mean the same thing to the modern believer as it did for the ancient writer who knew well the various codes of Law existing in the Pentateuch. But both ancient and modern believers are alike in agreeing that God's will for them is of supreme importance, a matter of meditation and joy. This suggestion opens the way for an appropriation of Torah in a new and different context. One can move with a broader understanding of Torah and allow oneself to be asked challenging questions: What is the will of God? How is it the subject of joyous meditation "day and night"? What is to be said about the contrasting fate of the righteous and wicked?

● This interpretation is guided by the assumption that there is a continuity, even where there are differences, between the Testaments. Readers with other presuppositions will interpret differently.

A gate-liturgy: Psalm 15 (cf. Psalm 24)

1 O Lord, who shall sojourn in thy tent?
   Who shall dwell on thy holy hill?

2 He who walks blamelessly, and does what is right,
   and speaks truth from his heart;
3 who does not slander with his tongue,
   and does no evil to his friend,
   nor takes up a reproach against his neighbor;
4 in whose eyes a reprobate is despised,
   but who honors those who fear the Lord;
   who swears to his own hurt and does not change;
5 who does not put out his money at interest,
   and does not take a bribe against the innocent.

He who does these things shall never be moved.

Psalm 15 exemplifies a type of "gate-liturgy," i.e., it contains the question/answer ritual that a worshiper enacted when entering the temple (cf. also Ps 118:19-20; Isa 33:14-16).

Structure. The question and answer determine the structure of the psalm. It is an exchange between personnel and a group of worshipers who have come to the temple. It was the task of the priest to indicate what was required to enter the presence of the deity. It was thought dangerous for anyone, especially the wicked, to dare to come before the Lord (Isa 33:14-16), and hence proclamation is made concerning the requisite qualities of the worshiper (cf. Jer 7:2-15; Mic 6:6-8).

Text. "Tent" and "hill" in v 1 are clear allusions to the

Jerusalem temple which succeeded to the desert tent, and was built on the Lord's holy mountain (cf. Exod 15:17). The description of the just person is expressed in general terms (v 2), and then a few particular ideals are specified. It is worthy of note that they refer to correct relationship with fellow human beings. The summary line certifies the person as a true worshiper (with the nuance of prosperity as in Ps 30:6).

Meaning. How is this ritual to be understood, both then and today? It would be a mistake to interpret it as though the Israelite worshiper had to be sinless in order to enter the temple. Nor should assumption of ability to enter be seen as a prideful claim. Rather, the ritual served as a *warning* of the awe and even trepidation with which a creature should come into the divine presence. It was also a profession of loyalty and dedication to the Lord who had specified what kind of worshipers was desired (vv 2-5; cf. Ezek 18:5-9). It states an ideal to be pursued.

● If one assumes that God's requirements are unchanging, then the text's question is appropriate for today's worshiper. What is the spirit, the quality, of one's worship of God? The need for ideals that correspond to God's will still remains, if worship is to be sincere. The concern about monetary "interest" (v 5) was significant in Israelite society (Deut 23:19-20). Even if present societal practice differs, the modern reader can profitably adapt this concern for neighbor in a responsible way; there is a continuity one can draw between ideals of righteousness then and now. It should not be difficult for an enlightened human conscience to transfer into a modern setting the point made by this psalm.

Lament of an individual: Psalm 22

1   My God, my God, why hast thou forsaken me?
     Why art thou so far from helping me, from the words of my
          groaning?

2 O my God, I cry by day, but thou dost not answer;
　　and by night, but find no rest.

3 Yet thou are holy,
　　enthroned on the praises of Israel.

4 In thee our fathers trusted;
　　they trusted, and thou didst deliver them.

5 To thee they cried, and were saved;
　　in thee they trusted, and were not disappointed.

6 But I am a worm, and no man;
　　scorned by men, and despised by the people.

7 All who see me mock at me,
　　they make mouths at me, they wag their heads;

8 "He committed his cause to the Lord; let him deliver him,
　　let him rescue him, for he delights in him!"

9 Yet thou art he who took me from the womb;
　　thou didst keep me safe upon my mother's breasts.

10 Upon thee was I cast from my birth,
　　and since my mother bore me thou hast been my God.

11 Be not far from me,
　　for trouble is near
　　and there is none to help.

12 Many bulls encompass me,
　　strong bulls of Bashan surround me;

13 they open wide their mouths at me,
　　like a ravening and roaring lion.

14 I am poured out like water,
　　and all my bones are out of joint;
　　my heart is like wax,
　　it is melted within my breast;

15 my strength is dried up like a potsherd,
　　and my tongue cleaves to my jaws;
　　thou dost lay me in the dust of death.

16 Yea, dogs are round about me;

a company of evildoers encircle me;
they have pierced my hands and feet—

17 I can count all my bones—
they stare and gloat over me;

18 they divide my garments among them,
and for my raiment they cast lots.

19 But thou, O Lord, be not far off!
O thou my help, hasten to my aid!

20 Deliver my soul from the sword,
my life from the power of the dog!

21 Save me from the mouth of the lion,
my afflicted soul from the horns of the wild oxen!

22 I will tell of thy name to my brethren;
in the midst of the congregation I will praise thee:

23 You who fear the Lord, praise him!
all you sons of Jacob, glorify him,
and stand in awe of him, all you sons of Israel!

24 For he has not despised or abhorred
the affliction of the afflicted;
and he has not hid his face from him,
but has heard, when he cried to him.

25 From thee comes my praise in the great congregation;
my vows I will pay before those who fear him.

26 The afflicted shall eat and be satisfied;
those who seek him shall praise the Lord!
May your hearts live for ever!

27 All the ends of the earth shall remember
and turn to the Lord;
and all the families of the nations
shall worship before him.

28 For dominion belongs to the Lord,
and he rules over the nations.

29 Yea, to him shall all the proud of the earth bow down;

> before him shall bow all who go down to the dust,
> and he who cannot keep himself alive.
> 30 Posterity shall serve him;
> men shall tell of the Lord to the coming generation,
> 31 and proclaim his deliverance to a people yet unborn,
> that he has wrought it.

Structure. In vv 1-21 is a clear lament of an individual, with repeated requests for deliverance, a description of distress, and motifs of confidence (vv 3-5, 9-11). In vv 22-31 the psalmist expresses thanksgiving for deliverance, and a community is invited to participate in this (vv 22-26); worldwide worship of the Lord is proclaimed (vv 27-31). The individual (as opposed to the collective) lament is the most frequent type of psalm in the Psalter. Its basic motifs are easily grasped: a cry to the Lord for help, a description of the psalmist's plight, reasons why the Lord should intervene (trust, loyalty), and finally a note of praise with the assurance that the prayer has been heard.

Terms. Many readers may be puzzled by the range and character of the images used to describe the psalmist's suffering: bulls of Bashan, dogs, lions, the sword—not to mention bones, throat, and heart. What exactly is the situation? Despite the detailed description, we are unable to pinpoint the particular suffering that gave rise to it; the symbols are entirely too broad for this.

● Paradoxically, this is a gain for the reader. If the author had truly described the situation in all its details, the prayer would have lost its universality and applicability to others. As it stands, the imagery is broad enough for all to utilize it as symbolic of their own suffering. The images are perhaps strange but nonetheless intelligible, and they answer the needs of all who suffer. The reader will find it useful to have recourse to a commentary or biblical dictionary for the nuances of certain images.

The last portion of the psalm (vv 22-31) contrasts so markedly with the complaint that many scholars have suspected that a thanksgiving psalm has been placed here editorially. In any case, themes of praise for the Lord's intervention, a thanksgiving banquet, and universalism (v 27, "all the ends of the earth") emerge, as the author contemplates his deliverance.

Meaning. Only a broad perspective can be offered here. At least three questions are worth considering. The first has already been indicated: the symbols used in the psalm. It is necessary to enter into the thought world of the psalmist in order to appreciate this imagery and its applicability to a personal situation. Second, there is the striking movement from lament to praise. This provides the context for the lament. No matter how violent and extravagant the language, it is voiced in the context of faith and trust in God. Walter Brueggemann has called attention to how this gives "formfulness" to grief. (See *Interpretation* 31 [1977] 263-75.) Grief need not be a permanent condition; one must move on to praise (the often mysterious) God. Finally the use of this psalm in the passion narratives (Matt 27:46; Mark 15:34), where the first verse is put on the lips of Jesus, will not go unnoticed by the Christian reader. There is no need to interpret this prayer as a prediction. It makes perfect sense as the prayer of a suffering Israelite. However, the use of the psalm in the NT tradition is surely creative and suggestive. It brings home to the Christian reader various dimensions of Christ's life: his knowledge of the OT; the prayers that nourished his own spirituality; and the movement from suffering to praise, from defeat to triumph, which Christians find in the crucifixion and resurrection.

Psalm of trust: Psalm 23

1   The Lord is my shepherd, I shall not want;
2   he makes me lie down in green pastures.

He leads me beside still waters;
3   he restores my soul.
He leads me in paths of righteousness
       for his name's sake.

4   Even though I walk through the valley of the shadow of death,
       I fear no evil;
     for thou art with me;
       thy rod and thy staff,
       they comfort me.

5   Thou preparest a table before me
       in the presence of my enemies;
     thou anointest my head with oil,
       my cup overflows.
6   Surely goodness and mercy shall follow me
       all the days of my life;
     and I shall dwell in the house of the Lord
       for ever.

Structure. The psalms of trust (16, 23, 62, 91, 125) seem to be a development of the note of trust with which psalms of lament include. It is as if this motif were made into a prayer of its own. The structure of Psalm 23 is simple: the presence of the Lord as a shepherd assures the psalmist of safety against any odds (vv 1-4); the sustenance provided by the Lord as banquet-host brings intimacy and security (vv 5-6).

Terms. "Shepherd" is the key image in the poem, and it reflects the ancient notion of kings as shepherds of their people. This is found elsewhere in the Bible (Isa 40:11; Ezekiel 34; John 10). The metaphor is developed in terms of pasturing the sheep, and there is a gradual movement in vv 2-4 from the metaphor to the concrete assistance the psalmist has received (and always relies on) from the shepherd. The famous phrase, "the valley of the shadow of death" *(ṣēl māwet)* should probably be rendered

as "the dark valley" *(şalmût),* a more appropriate image for
sheep out in the pasture.

The cup and oil (v 5) point to the hospitable banquet
provided by the Lord. This may be considered literally as a
sacred meal in the "house of the Lord," or temple, which is
mentioned in v 6; but it can also serve as a metaphor for the total
care that the psalmist has received. The phrase, "for ever"
(v 6), merely means a period of indefinite duration.

Meaning. The interpretation is easily guided by the mood and
metaphors of shepherd and host. We cannot particularize the
specific experiences of the psalmist which prompted this prayer.
Needless to say, countless biblical readers have judged that it is
also applicable to them. Either they have had an experience
similar to that of the psalmist, or they aspire to it.

Psalm of thanksgiving: Psalm 30

1 I will extol thee, O Lord, for thou has drawn me up,
    and hast not let my foes rejoice over me.
2 O Lord my God, I cried to thee for help,
    and thou hast healed me.
3 O Lord, thou hast brought up my soul from Sheol,
    restored me to life from among those gone down to the Pit.

4 Sing praises to the Lord, O you his saints,
    and give thanks to his holy name.
5 For his anger is but for a moment,
    and his favor is for a lifetime.
  Weeping may tarry for the night,
    but joy comes with the morning.

6 As for me, I said in my prosperity,
    "I shall never be moved."
7 By thy favor, O Lord,
    thou hadst established me as a strong mountain;
  thou didst hide thy face,
    I was dismayed.

8   To thee, O Lord, I cried;
        and to the Lord I made supplication:
9   "What profit is there in my death,
        if I go down to the Pit?
    Will the dust praise thee?
        Will it tell of thy faithfulness?
10 Hear, O Lord, and be gracious to me!
        O Lord, be thou my helper!"

11 Thou hast turned for me my mourning into dancing;
        thou hast loosed my sackcloth
        and girded me with gladness,
12 that my soul may praise thee and not be silent.
        O Lord my God, I will give thanks to thee for ever.

Structure. Thanksgiving is not easy to distinguish from praise, as this poem illustrates. It begins in the style of a hymn or song of praise (v 1), but it has certain characteristic features: the acknowledgement of the Lord as the rescuer (vv 2-3) and the public witness to this (vv 4-5) as the author urges the bystanders—who will share also in the sacrificial meal that his prayer accompanies—to join him in praise. It is as if he were to say: what happened to me can happen to you. A flashback (vv 6-10) tells how the life of the complacent psalmist was disrupted by some trial (never specified), and of his prayer in the throes of his distress. The conclusion reverts to the Lord's intervention and ends on a note of praise.

Terms. The notion of Sheol or the Pit has been explained elsewhere (see the exegesis of Sirach 41 in chapter 3). The psalmist does not mean that he has literally come back from Sheol. The word is used as metaphor for the distress, the experience of nonlife, from which he was delivered. There is a small "sermon" delivered to the bystanders in v 5. The bad turn in his life is expressed in the vivid phrase of the Lord hiding his face (cf. Ps 104:29). The prayer uttered in this period is a simple one: keep me alive that I may sing your praises, because I will not be able to do so when I am dead. This underlines another aspect of Sheol. Not only is it a bleak existence (cf. Eccl 9:10), a kind of nonlife, but there is no loving contact with the Lord.

Meaning. The universality, and hence applicability, of this psalm is manifest: gratitude to God for deliverance from distress. The metaphorical use of Sheol is a manner of expression, an insight into death, that one can readily appreciate. By "life" is meant of course the good life: prosperity and blessing, as the Wisdom Literature and the Psalms make evident. But, one may ask, when is one most alive? The answer is reached by contemplating life's opposite: Sheol. This is characterized as a place where one can no longer praise God (cf. also Ps 6:5), and where one is *most dead,* as it were. The answer to being "most alive" then emerges by opposition: when one praises God. As the German phrase has it, *Leben ist loben;* "to live is to praise."

Hymn (to Zion): Psalm 48

1   Great is the Lord and greatly to be praised
    in the city of our God!
  His holy mountain, 2 beautiful in elevation,
    is the joy of all the earth,
  Mount Zion, in the far north,
    the city of the great King.
3   Within her citadels God
    has shown himself a sure defense.

4   For lo, the kings assembled,
    they came on together.
5   As soon as they saw it, they were astonished,

they were in panic, they took to flight;
6   trembling took hold of them there,
        anguish as of a woman in travail.
7   By the east wind thou didst shatter
        the ships of Tarshish.
8   As we have heard, so have we seen
        in the city of the Lord of hosts,
      in the city of our God,
        which God establishes for ever. *Selah*

9   We have thought on thy steadfast love, O God,
        in the midst of thy temple.
10 As thy name, O God,
        so thy praise reaches to the ends of the earth.
    Thy right hand is filled with victory;
11   let Mount Zion be glad!
    Let the daughters of Judah rejoice
        because of thy judgments!

12 Walk about Zion, go round about her,
        number her towers,
13 consider well her ramparts,
        go through her citadels;
    that you may tell the next generation
14   that this is God,
    our God for ever and ever,
        He will be our guide for ever.

A hymn is essentially a song of praise. The psalmist usually
begins on a joyous note, urging a group (or even, self, as in
Psalms 103, 104), to exult, rejoice, to praise the Lord. Then
follows the *reason* for the praise: God's creative activity and/or
his saving intervention in Israel's history. After the development of these themes the hymn may return to its opening
appeal. In view of the content, many songs of praise can be

further classified as hymns of Zion (Jerusalem is the object of praise) or hymns of the Lord's kingship ("The Lord is king!").

Structure. Although it lacks the customary invocation to rejoice, the psalm presents an object of praise and admiration, namely Zion, "the city of our God." Because of Jerusalem's association with the Lord there is no title, however extravagant, that cannot be applied to her (vv 1-3). The next strophe describes (in an imaginative fashion?) an assault by her enemies who go down to defeat (vv 4-7). Strophe three is the grateful reflection of Jerusalem's citizens on the protection and kindness of the Lord to Jerusalem (vv 8-11). The final strophe (vv 12-14) is a boast, an invitation to inspect the city and its walls. It is impregnable because of the presence of God therein.

Terms. There are certain nuances to the phrases describing Zion that deserve attention. "In the far north" implicitly compares Jerusalem to Mt. Saphon near ancient Ugarit, which was the residence of the Canaanite pantheon (cf. Mt. Olympus in Greek mythology). The "great king" is a phrase appearing frequently in Akkadian literature to designate the powerful Mesopotamian monarchs. Although Tarshish remains unidentified (probably somewhere in the Mediterranean?), the reference is to large, seagoing ships. *Selah* is a famous term which occurs many times in the Psalter, and its meaning has never been successfully explained. By the "judgments" of v 11 are meant the saving intervention of the Lord.

Meaning. This song will not be properly appreciated if the association between the Lord and Zion is not truly understood. The praise of Jerusalem is felt and expressed in a human and patriotic way; great pride is taken in the city. But this is because it is where God (or his Name, as Deuteronomy prefers to put it) dwells. One must not lose sight of this glory of Jerusalem, which derives from the divine presence. Such a view of Zion is reflected frequently in the Bible (Isaiah 60–62; Ezekiel 47–48;

and cf. Revelation 21–22). The theme of the invincibility of
Zion occurs especially in Isa 14:32; 29:8; 31; 37).

> ● On the topic of Jerusalem an interesting dialectic develops
> within the OT. Side by side with the praise of Jerusalem is the
> prophetic indictment of her people who seek a false security in
> the "city of God." Such an indictment is mounted even by Isaiah
> (1:21-31; 3:1–4:1), and especially by Jeremiah (7:1-15; 24:1-10;
> 26:1-19). A rallying cry in one generation becomes a trap in
> another generation. The confidence which this psalm expresses
> is therefore not to be absolutized. The psalm is to be read in the
> light of this dialectic about the Holy City.

In medieval exegesis, "Jerusalem" was commonly used to
illustrate the various senses of Scripture; in the literal sense, it
was the city in Palestine; in the allegorical sense (a hidden
theological meaning), it was the church; in the anagogical (or
mystical sense), it was the heavenly home to which one is to
tend; and finally in the moral sense, Jerusalem is the individual
soul and its behavior. At least some of these senses appear in
Paul's complicated theological construction in Gal 4:22-31.

A hymn: Psalm 117

1 Praise the Lord, all nations!
    Extol him, all peoples!
2 For great is his steadfast love toward us;
    and the faithfulness of the Lord endures for ever.
    Praise the Lord!

Structure. This is the shortest psalm, and it illustrates the
basic structure of the hymn: an invitation to praise the Lord,
followed by the reason for praise.

Terms. The importance of knowing the nuances of certain
key words appears in this short prayer. "Steadfast love" *(ḥesed)*

is the bond of love, emerging from the covenant, which the Lord has for the people. "Faithfulness" *('emet)* is that quality of the Lord that makes the divine promises (e.g., to the patriarchs) reliable.

Meaning. The above remarks concerning *ḥesed* and *'emet* are important for Israel's self-understanding. The theology of the OT rests, in considerable measure, on these two pillars.

● They continue to be important to those who identify with the people of God and thus understand themselves as benefiting from the divine promises (Luke 1:68-79). Faithfulness to his promises is a fundamental trait of the Lord (cf. Isa 40:8).

Lament of the community: Psalm 74

1 O God, why dost thou cast us off for ever?
     Why does thy anger smoke against the sheep of thy pasture?
2 Remember thy congregation, which thou hast gotten of old,
        which thou hast redeemed to be the tribe of thy heritage!
        Remember Mount Zion, where thou hast dwelt.
3 Direct thy steps to the perpetual ruins;
        the enemy has destroyed everything in the sanctuary!

4 Thy foes have roared in the midst of thy holy place;
        they set up their own signs for signs.
5 At the upper entrance they hacked
        the wooden trellis with axes.
6 And then all its carved wood
        they broke down with hatchets and hammers.
7 They set thy sanctuary on fire;
        to the ground they desecrated the dwelling place of thy name.
8 They said to themselves, "We will utterly subdue them";
        they burned all the meeting places of God in the land.

9 We do not see our signs;
        there is no longer any prophet,

and there is none among us who knows how long.
10 How long, O God, is the foe to scoff?
    Is the enemy to revile thy name for ever?
11 Why dost thou hold back thy hand,
    why dost thou keep thy right hand in thy bosom?

12 Yet God my King is from of old,
    working salvation in the midst of the earth.
13 Thou didst divide the sea by thy might;
    thou didst break the heads of the dragons on the waters.
14 Thou didst crush the heads of Leviathan,
    thou didst give him as food for the creatures of the
       wilderness.
15 Thou didst cleave open springs and brooks;
    thou didst dry up ever-flowing streams.
16 Thine is the day, thine also the night;
    thou hast established the luminaries and the sun.
17 Thou hast fixed all the bounds of the earth;
    thou has made summer and winter.

18 Remember this, O Lord, how the enemy scoffs,
    and an impious people reviles thy name.
19 Do not deliver the soul of thy dove to the wild beasts;
    do not forget the life of thy poor for ever.

20 Have regard for thy covenant;
    for the dark places of the land are full of the habitations of
       violence.
21 Let not the downtrodden be put to shame;
    let the poor and needy praise thy name.

22 Arise, O God, plead thy cause;
    remember how the impious scoff at thee all the day!
23 Do not forget the clamor of thy foes,
    the uproar of thy adversaries which goes up continually!

Structure. The movement within the collective lament is generally the same as within the individual lament. The appeal for help is disguised in the opening question, Why? and a description of the situation follows (vv 1-11). A small hymn in praise of the Lord as creator is found in vv 12-17. The prayer ends with appeals and reminders addressed to God. The occasion seems to be a devastation of the sanctuary (vv 3-8), but the date, perhaps 598 or 587 B.C., is impossible to determine exactly.

Terms. The nuances in "thy congregation, "the tribe of thy heritage," "Mount Zion, where thou hast dwelt," should be noted. These words are loaded; how is it possible for the Lord to neglect the people who are so closely identified with him? The portrayal of the damage to the temple is likewise aimed at moving the Lord to intervene.

The hymnic development about divine power serves as a reminder to the Lord that he *can,* if he will. It is interesting that creation is viewed as God's "working salvation" (v 12). The act of creation is portrayed in the mythical language which we know from OT poetry. Creation is conceived of as a victory over chaos—the sea *(Yam),* the dragons and Leviathan (cf. Ps 89:10; Isa 27:1).

The motifs that should induce intervention point to God's own honor: the scoffing of the enemy, the covenant, care for the poor and needy. The psalm ends with a ringing summons to the Lord to arise and remember (this is more than a mere act of memory!).

Meaning. The above analysis conveys some sense of the historical meaning which the psalm must have had for ancient Israel. It is surely significant that such communal complaints (see also Psalms 44, 60, 79, 80, 83, 94:1-7, 123) were preserved and finally entered the selected writings of Israel. They were a steady reminder of past troubles, but also of the Lord's assistance; after all, the people of God continued on their mission.

What does such a psalm have to say to a reader of the Bible in the modern era? First, one may ask whether our prayer is truly communal or highly privatized. True, the average church/synagogue experience includes communal prayers, but this fact leaves untouched the sense of community that should bind believers together. There is no prescribed degree of "(comm)unity" in this matter, but the underlying question is one of identity, Who are we as the worshiping community: What is our relationship to suffering Israel? This psalm challenges the highly individualistic style that characterizes modern religion and culture and it forces us to rethink our spiritual roots in Israel.

The modern reader may judge the concern of this psalm, the destruction of Zion, less than compelling. But one can learn to appreciate the significance of Zion as the privileged place of divine presence. The sense of "holy space," which Israel celebrated, is almost lost in the modern world. Perhaps we have not lost appreciation of the indomitable faith of a people that was bold enough to call the Lord to account concerning his responsibility (v 20, "have regard for thy covenant!"). This lament does not provide the final word on divine presence or covenant, but it challenges us to take them seriously within our own religious perspective.

Royal psalm: Psalm 89

1   I will sing of thy steadfast love, O Lord, for ever;
        with my mouth I will proclaim thy faithfulness to all
        generations.
2   For thy steadfast love was established for ever,
        thy faithfulness is firm as the heavens.
3   Thou hast said, "I have made a covenant with my chosen one,
        I have sworn to David my servant:

4 'I will establish your descendants for ever,
    and build your throne for all generations.'" *Selah*

5 Let the heavens praise thy wonders, O Lord,
    thy faithfulness in the assembly of the holy ones!

6 For who in the skies can be compared to the Lord?
    Who among the sons of god is like the Lord?

7 a God feared in the council of the holy ones,
    great and terrible above all that are round about him?

8 O Lord God of hosts,
    who is mighty as thou art, O Lord,
    with thy faithfulness found about thee?

9 Thou dost rule the raging of the sea;
    when its waves rise, thou stillest them.

10 Thou didst crush Rahab like a carcass,
    thou didst scatter thy enemies with thy mighty arm.

11 The heavens are thine, the earth also is thine;
    the world and all that is in it, thou hast founded them. . . .

38 But now thou hast cast off and rejected,
    thou are full of wrath against thy anointed.

39 Thou hast renounced the covenant with thy servant;
    thou has defiled his crown in the dust. . . .

46 How long, O Lord? Wilt thou hide thyself for ever?
    How long will thy wrath burn like fire? . . .

49 Lord, where is thy steadfast love of old,
    which by thy faithfulness thou didst swear to David? . . .

52 Blessed be the Lord for ever!
    Amen and Amen.

Structure. For our purposes, the psalm has been excerpted. But enough is reproduced (vv 1-11, 38-39, 46, 49, 52) to make clear how unusual this prayer is. In terms of its main theme, this is a royal psalm, in which the author rehearses the covenant of the Lord with David (2 Samuel 7). This theme is introduced as a sign of the "steadfast love" and "faithfulness" of the Lord (v 1; cf. Psalm 117 above). Then there is a sudden switch to a hymnlike development of the uniqueness of the Lord because of his creative activity (vv 8-18). After this apparent digression the psalm returns to the topic of the covenant with David (vv 19-37). Then, in the style of a complaint, the psalmist accuses the Lord of failing to keep the covenant: the royal descendant of David has been cast off (vv 38-45). "How long?" (v 46) is typical of a lament, and so is the motif of the shortness of life (vv 47-48). The psalm closes with an appeal to the Lord's steadfast love and faithfulness (v 49, which forms a literary inclusion with vv 1-2). The final verses (46-51) seem to be spoken by the king, or at least in his name. The last verse is a doxology which ends the third of the five books into which the Psalter is divided; it is not part of the psalm.

This prayer has unusual characteristics: it begins like a hymn and ends like a lament; it centers on the Davidic covenant and elaborates the promises of the Lord to the dynasty, but it also incorporates a hymn to the Lord's creative power (cf. Ps 74:12-17). This hymn (vv 8-18) may once have been a separate psalm, but it makes sense in its present context.

Terms. The theological significance of "steadfast love" and "faithfulness" (vv 1-2, 8, 14, 28, 33, 49) has already been pointed out in the treatment of Psalm 117 above. The covenant with David (vv 19-37) refers to the divine promise that a descendant of David would always reign from Jerusalem (2 Samuel 7). Even if the members of the dynasty prove unfaithful and are punished, the Lord will not go back on his word.

Three items of note form the background of the praise offered in vv 5-14: the heavenly court, the worship of the Yahweh alone, and the description of creation. The Lord was conceived as dwelling above the blue firmament with the sons of

God (v 6), or "heavenly beings" who constitute the divine court (see the analysis of Job 1:6-12 above). Their function was to praise the Lord (Psalm 29) and to carry out his will (as "angels," or messengers). Here the incomparability of the Lord is celebrated. None of these Elohim-beings (or, sons of El) can match him. One should note that their divine nature poses no problem for the psalmist. The existence of divine beings is taken for granted. But there is only *one* Yahweh, absolute and superior to them all (vv 6-7). This is practical, not theoretical monotheism: a "mono-Yahwism," as it has been called. The Lord's superiority is rooted in his creative activity. This is portrayed as a conflict with the powers of chaos, represented by the "sea" (v 9; cf. Ps 74:13) and personified in Rahab (v 10; cf. Leviathan in Pss 74:14; 104:26), an unruly monster of the deep. This conflict between the Lord and chaos is another mode of describing his creative activity (cf. Gen 1:2).

Meaning. This psalm presents at least two theological issues for us to ponder: monotheism and the fidelity of the Lord to his promises. Monotheism is so easily taken for granted in the Western world. In the ancient Near East a comfortable polytheism existed, and it was only gradually that Israel came to the understanding that the exclusive worship of the Lord alone ultimately rested on a monotheistic understanding. In Deutero-Isaiah other gods go down in defeat (Isaiah 46); they are called "godlings," or "nothings" *('elîlîm)*. According to Ps 115:5 the idols "have mouths, but do not speak; eyes, but do not see." The next logical step, once their inefficacious activity is understood, is the rejection of their very existence.

The Davidic covenant is held up before the Lord in a manner that is loving, but also accusatory. Where does the Lord stand, ultimately? His fidelity is recognized, but there is the inevitable question, How does it square with the facts? We cannot be sure of the date of this psalm—does it refer to Hezekiah, "caged like

a bird, in Jerusalem" under Sennacherib's siege in 701, or to
Josiah slain at Megiddo in 609, or even to the fall of Jerusalem
in 587? If the historical reference remains uncertain, the
theological issue does not, and it emerged all through Israel's
existence as a people, as Genesis 22 (the testing of Abraham)
reminds us. How is one to understand divine "faithfulness" in
the context of a history which seems to negate it? How much
freedom does the Lord have in keeping his word?

A song of ascents: Psalm 130

1 Out of the depths I cry to thee, O Lord!
2   Lord, hear my voice!
   Let thy ears be attentive
      to the voice of my supplications!

3 If thou, O Lord, shouldst mark iniquities,
      Lord, who could stand?
4 But there is forgiveness with thee,
      that thou mayest be feared.

5 I wait for the Lord, my soul waits,
      and in his word I hope;
6 my soul waits for the Lord
      more than watchmen for the morning.
      more than watchmen for the morning.

7 O Israel, hope in the Lord!
      For with the Lord there is steadfast love,
      and with him is plenteous redemption.
 8 And he will redeem Israel
      from all his iniquities.

Structure. This famous psalm belongs in the group entitled
"Songs of Ascent" (Psalms 120–134). One can only guess at the
reason for this title. It is thought that they were songs which
pilgrims uttered as they "went up" to Jerusalem, or that they

sang on the fifteen steps going up into the sanctuary of the Israelites in the temple. Others point to the "step," or "staircase" parallelism that characterizes many of these prayers (e.g., Ps 121:3-4, 7-8). Psalm 130 is a lament of an individual, although it includes the people at the finale. As usual, the beginning is a cry for deliverance (vv 1-2), and it is followed by an appeal to the Lord's mercy (vv 3-4), and the motif of trust (vv 6-7). The final verses address the community in a kind of generalization of the psalmist's experience.

Terms. The "depths" are the depths of Sheol, which is used metaphorically here for the psalmist's distress (cf. Ps 30:3). It is the Lord's readiness to forgive that prompts this prayer. What is the "word" in which the speaker hopes so ardently (v 5)? Perhaps it is an oracle of salvation, a divine word of encouragement pronounced by one of the temple personnel.

Meaning. This brief prayer stands out by its succinct characterization of the human condition: personal distress, reliance upon divine mercy, hope, the association of the individual with the community. These are values that a people, in continuity with the people of God, can adopt with profit.

Wisdom psalm: Psalm 37

1 Fret not yourself because of the wicked,
    be not envious of wrongdoers!

2 For they will soon fade like the grass,
    and wither like the green herb.

3 Trust in the Lord, and do good;
    so you will dwell in the land, and enjoy security.

4 Take delight in the Lord,
    and he will give you the desires of your heart.

5 Commit your way to the Lord;
    trust in him, and he will act.

6　He will bring forth your vindication as the light,
and your right as the noonday.

7　Be still before the Lord, and wait patiently for him;
fret not yourself over him who prospers in his way,
over the man who carries out evil devices!

8　Refrain from anger, and forsake wrath!
Fret not yourself; it tends only to evil.

9　For the wicked shall be cut off;
but those who wait for the Lord shall possess the land.

10　Yet a little while, and the wicked will be no more;
though you look well at his place, he will not be there.

11　But the meek shall possess the land,
and delight themselves in abundant prosperity.

12　The wicked plots against the righteous,
and gnashes his teeth at him;

13　but the Lord laughs at the wicked,
for he sees that his day is coming.

14　The wicked draw the sword and bend their bows,
to bring down the poor and needy,
to slay those who walk uprightly;

15　their sword shall enter their own heart,
and their bows shall be broken.

16　Better is a little that the righteous has
than the abundance of many wicked,

17　For the arms of the wicked shall be broken;
but the Lord upholds the righteous.

18　The Lord knows the days of the blameless,
and their heritage will abide for ever;

19　they are not put to shame in evil times,
in the days of famine they have abundance.

20　But the wicked perish;
the enemies of the Lord are like the glory of the pastures,
they vanish—like smoke they vanish away.

21 The wicked borrows, and cannot pay back,
    but the righteous is generous and gives;
22 for those blessed by the Lord shall possess the land,
    but those cursed by him shall be cut off.

23 The steps of a man are from the Lord,
    and he establishes him in whose way he delights;
24 though he fall, he shall not be cast headlong.
    for the Lord is the stay of his hand.

25 I have been young, and now am old;
    yet I have not seen the righteous forsaken
    or his children begging bread.
26 He is ever giving liberally and lending,
    and his children become a blessing.

27 Depart from evil, and do good;
    so shall you abide for ever.
28 For the Lord loves justice;
    he will not forsake his saints.

    The righteous shall be preserved for ever,
    but the children of the wicked shall be cut off.
29 The righteous shall possess the land,
    and dwell upon it for ever.

30 The mouth of the righteous utters wisdom,
    and his tongue speaks justice.
31 The law of his God is in his heart;
    his steps do not slip.

32 The wicked watches the righteous,
    and seeks to slay him.
33 The Lord will not abandon him to his power,
    or let him be condemned when he is brought to trial.

34 Wait for the Lord, and keep to his way,
    and he will exalt you to possess the land;
    you will look on the destruction of the wicked.

35 I have seen a wicked man overbearing,
   and towering like a cedar of Lebanon.

36 Again I passed by, and lo, he was no more;
   though I sought him, he could not be found.

37 Mark the blameless man, and behold the upright,
   for there is posterity for the man of peace.

38 But transgressors shall be altogether destroyed;
   the posterity of the wicked shall be cut off.

39 The salvation of the righteous is from the Lord;
   he is their refuge in the time of trouble.

40 The Lord helps them and delivers them;
   he delivers them from the wicked, and saves them,
   because they take refuge in him.

Wisdom psalm: Psalm 73

1 Truly God is good to the upright,
   to those who are pure in heart.

2 But as for me, my feet had almost stumbled,
   my steps had well nigh slipped.

3 For I was envious of the arrogant,
   when I saw the prosperity of the wicked.

4 For they have no pangs;
   their bodies are sound and sleek.

5 They are not in trouble as other men are;
   they are not stricken like other men.

6 Therefore pride is their necklace;
   violence covers them as a garment.

7 Their eyes swell out with fatness,
   their hearts overflow with follies.

8 They scoff and speak with malice;
   loftily they threaten oppression.

9 They set their mouths against the heavens,
   and their tongue struts through the earth.

10 Therefore the people turn and praise them,
   and find no fault in them.

11 And they say, "How can God know?
   Is there knowledge in the Most High?"
12 Behold, these are the wicked;
   always at ease, they increase in riches.
13 All in vain have I kept my heart clean
   and washed my hands in innocence.
14 For all the day long I have been stricken,
   and chastened every morning.

15 If I had said, "I will speak thus,"
   I would have been untrue to the generation of thy children.
16 But when I thought how to understand this,
   it seemed to me a wearisome task,
17 until I went into the sanctuary of God;
   then I perceived their end.
18 Truly thou dost set them in slippery places;
   thou dost make them fall to ruin.
19 How they are destroyed in a moment,
   swept away utterly by terrors!
20 They are like a dream when one awakes,
   on awaking you despise their phantoms.

21 When my soul was embittered,
   when I was pricked in heart,
22 I was stupid and ignorant,
   I was like a beast toward thee.
23 Nevertheless I am continually with thee;
   thou dost hold my right hand.
24 Thou dost guide me with thy counsel,
   and afterward thou wilt receive me to glory.
25 Whom have I in heaven but thee?
   And there is nothing upon earth that I desire besides thee.
26 My flesh and my heart may fail,
   but God is the strength of my heart and my portion for ever.

27 For lo, those who are far from thee shall perish;
   thou dost put an end to those who are false to thee.

28 But for me it is good to be near God;
I have made the Lord God my refuge,
that I may tell of all thy works.

The classification, "wisdom psalms," is a rather questionable one, not as clearly definable as are hymns, laments, and other types. Yet certain psalms betray themes and characteristics of the forms that are popular in Wisdom Literature, such as admonitions, "better"-sayings, comparisons, "blessed"-sayings, alphabetic structure. There is no unanimous opinion, but the reader might consider reading Psalms 32, 34, 49, 111, 112, 128 in this light. If there is no strict literary type that can be termed sapiential, then at least several psalms betray wisdom influence. The choice of Psalms 37 and 73 for treatment here is suggested by the very differences that exist between them. Yet they can be considered as relevant to wisdom.

Structure. The structure of Psalm 37 is that of an acrostic, i.e., each verse opens with an initial letter that follows the sequence of the Hebrew alphabet. Thus there is little logical sequence in the succession of sayings, commands, and admonitions that follow one another. The psalmist begins with a problem: the temptation which the good person has to envy the prosperity of the wicked. He applies all the wisdom he can to assuring the addressee (addressed in the singular) that God will intervene in favor of the one who trusts in him.

Terms. The comparisons are simple enough; thus the "cedar of Lebanon" is a symbol of a proud man. The vividness of the language should be noted: the sword and bow of the wicked (v 14), borrowing and lending (v 21), the experience of the elderly psalmist (v 26), the emphasis on the land (vv 3, 9, 11, 22, 29, 34). The teaching of the psalmist is quite clear: there is no reason to be upset about the course of the wicked; one should trust in the Lord who will intervene in favor of those who are

faithful to him. It is the just who will abide "for ever" (v 27—cf.
Ps 23:6, above; there is no notion of infinity here, merely
indefinite duration) and "possess the land." On the other hand,
the wicked will be destroyed (v 13, "his day is coming"—this is
not final judgment, but simply the day of reversal for the wicked
by reason of losing unjust gains or by premature death). It is
important to recognize the perspective of the psalmist: *this life;*
it is in the here and now that one will witness the justice of
God who intervenes in favor of those who "take refuge in him"
(v 40).

Meaning. It is only too easy for a modern reader to become
impatient with this psalm. For one thing, it is monotonous. The
author rings all the changes on the theme of divine retribution.
The style is consistently admonitory and expository, broadened
by motive clauses to support the teaching. Some verses would
fit easily into the Book of Proverbs (cf. the admonitions in
Prov 22:17–24:31). Moreover the psalm is not a prayer, but an
exhortation not to give up on God's ways with humans. The
advice that is offered is: trust in God! Surely, this cannot be
faulted; it is a fairly consistent theme throughout the Bible. It is
in the elaboration of the reasons for trusting in God that one
finds difficulty (e.g., vv 3-6, 9). The criterion applied to the
Lord is human justice; he will give prosperity to the just, while
the wicked will come to ruin. One wonders what kind of
sheltered person could write that he has never "seen the
righteous forsaken" (v 25). It would be easier to condemn the
injustice suffered by the righteous (and attributable to God,
vv 23-24). But instead of this the psalmist demands a blind trust
in the Lord's governance. Things may go awry, but this
condition cannot be permanent; in the end good will triumph.
This is a lofty vision, even paradoxical, which he urges on his
audience. If the Bible did not contain other voices that dispute
the theme of Psalm 37, the reader would be faced only with this

offer of blind faith (which, be it admitted, is genuinely biblical—the question is the degree of blindness).

● This psalm must be interpreted in the light of such books as Job and Ecclesiastes. Indeed, the doctrine of Psalm 37 is similar to the views of Job's three friends, of whom it is said "you have not spoken of me what is right" (Job 42:7). Psalm 37, then, represents a point of view addressed to tormented humanity, urging us to find our refuge in God. But its perspective is not a total one; the entire sweep of biblical thought (from Abraham to Job to Isaiah 53 to Christ) shows that reality is more complex than the author envisioned.

Psalm 73

Structure. From a literary point of view this psalm would be better classified as one of thanksgiving. This is the note that is sounded in v 1, (and cf. v 28), where the author gives witness to the Lord's goodness, a conclusion to which he has fought his way, as the rest of the psalm indicates. Because the theme is the divine treatment of the just and the unjust, many scholars consider this to be a wisdom psalm. It should be candidly admitted that this topic alone is not enough to constitute literary work as wisdom. Nonetheless, Psalm 73 deserves to be included here as an interesting companion piece to Psalm 37.

The opening verses (1-2) state the problem succinctly. The psalmist has been sorely tried, even to rebellion against God, by the prosperity which the wicked enjoy. There follows a description of the life-style of the wicked (vv 4-11), and the psalmist's personal crisis is over this "scandal," which was relieved only by a visit to the sanctuary (vv 12-17). There he came to understand that the wicked will perish and to appreciate his own stupidity (vv 18-22). In contrast to the treatment of the wicked, he describes his own fate: union with

God (vv 23-28), which issues in praise of him ("tell of all thy works").

Terms. The Hebrew text is uncertain at various points, but this does not affect the general meaning. Thus it makes little difference what reading one follows in v 1 (cf. the footnote in the RSV). One should not miss the gravity of the despair of the loyal psalmist who does what is right but only suffers for it (vv 13-14), and who flirts with deserting to the ranks of the wicked. It is only during a visit to the sanctuary (*miqdāsh,* which means the temple) that he comes to see their "end" (v 17, literally, "after"). What follows is the stereotype description of the fate of the wicked (vv 18-20); one wonders why the psalmist makes so much of this commonplace about the destruction of the wicked. On the other hand, his view of his own fate is described with ever-growing intensity: union with God. What did he mean here (vv 23-28)? The terms, "continually," "glory," "heaven," "receive," "for ever," do not necessarily connote a blessed immortality with God. Adverbs of time indicate merely indefinite duration; glory can be earthly; and "heaven" is clearly opposed to "earth," yielding two opposite poles to exhaust the range of the psalmist's desire. Hence the issue posed in these verses: Is the psalmist acknowledging God's care for him in this life, or is it in the next life, a kind of "intimation of immortality"? Scholars are divided on the point. In any case, the intense "I-thou" relationship described in vv 23-28 is unsurpassed in the Bible.

Meaning. Two issues deserve mention. The first is the struggle which the ancient Israelite experienced in the face of evildoing and the prosperity of the wicked. This is not only frequent in the Bible (cf. Job 21:7-34; Jer 12:1-5), but also a perennial theme in human experience and in literature. The struggle is vividly described, even though it was resolved by the time the psalmist composed the prayer.

The second issue is the personal solution at which the psalmist arrived. The traditional fate of the wicked is hardly a solution, even though it is stated. It is certainly not new; the author is borrowing a well-documented theme in the Bible. But he does not stop here; he goes on to consider his own fate: companionship with God. It matters little that there is uncertainty as to whether he refers to life with God after death (see above). The essential vision is clear: God holds him by the hand and guides him, gives him glory. This leads him to assert that God is his only real good, and nearness to God is everything. If there is no immortality here, the modern reader is challenged to determine what role God plays in his or her personal life in the here and now. Once more (cf. the exegesis of Wis 1:15 in chapter 3) we may need to purify our understanding of God and life.

EPILOGUE

1. How ready are we to trust the view of life which biblical wisdom recommends? We have seen that Lady Wisdom has many faces, ranging from observations about the "way it is," all the way to claims about her divine origin. Which aspect of "wisdom" speaks to us? We must recognize the movement that takes place within the wisdom tradition.

Two significant changes occur in the span of wisdom from Proverbs to the Wisdom of Solomon. One is the development of the figure of Lady Wisdom, which has been treated in the passages selected for exegesis. This tantalizing Lady never quite reveals her identity. Ben Sira, as we have seen, identified her with the Law. This move corresponded well to the piety of his time. The mystery of God's will and gracious guidance is not thereby exhausted. Wisdom is appropriated and identified as an ideal for the author's generation. The unidentified Jew of the Diaspora who was responsible for the Wisdom of Solomon recognized in her a gift of God, an intimacy with the Lord, a savior figure. The notion of wisdom as gift (cf. 1 Kgs 3:9 and Prov 2:6) is prolonged in the perspective of Paul, who sees in Christ the supreme gift, "wisdom of God" (1 Cor 1:24, 30). The development of wisdom in the patristic and medieval period and in the humanistic writings of the Renaissance is not part of our investigation, but it deserves mention as the prolongation of the journey that wisdom began in the ancient Near East.

The second item that calls for attention is the inner tensions attached to wisdom within the Bible. The proud and confident claims of the sages which the Book of Proverbs records, are succeeded by the tortured counterclaims registered in Job and Ecclesiastes. Does this sequence mark the "failure" and "bankruptcy" of wisdom? Rather, it attests the purification and disciplining of those who strive after wisdom. Wisdom would not be a divine gift if she came ready-made to human beings. She had to retain the mystery that her divine origin suggests. She speaks for God, and "how small a whisper do we hear of him!" (Job 26:14). Israel's literature elevated ancient Near Eastern wisdom to a divine quest, and all of us are somehow involved in the journey.

2. How open are we to the prayer of Israel as it is presented in the Psalms? It is a striking fact that this collection has been the prayer book par excellence of both Christianity and Judaism. Countless numbers have found strength and consolation, inspiration and insight, in the words of other people, the Psalms. Prayer is a uniquely personal thing, but the Psalms have provided a voice for all kinds of persons. Perhaps this is due primarily to the fact that death is confronted. As Christoph Barth observes,

> H. Gunkel says of the individual psalms of lamentation that they are "the place where the religion of the psalms comes into conflict with death." In a less well-known comment, O Noordmans says of this conflict that the psalms are the greatest of all the wonders of the world; for without giving any clear

knowledge of the nature of death, "they have helped one generation after another to pass through death."[1]

We have referred to the Psalter as a "school of prayer" in the sense that it can teach us how to pray. Identification with the psalmist and the words of the psalm expands our perspectives. The medieval practice of *lectio divina,* or listening to the Word of God, is also pertinent here. Simple contemplation of the ways of God with humans can facilitate a deeper level of responding to the Lord. The constant appearance of praise and joy in the Psalms transforms prayer from mere petition to a fuller awareness of divine presence. The lively response of the psalmist needs to be heard in our days: "to live is to praise."

[1]Christoph Barth, *Introduction to the Psalms,* trans. R. A. Wilson (New York: Charles Scribner's Sons, 1966), p. 49.

AIDS FOR THE INTERPRETER

Israel's Wisdom in General

W. Brueggemann, *In Man We Trust* (Atlanta: John Knox Press, 1972). Brueggemann describes an alternative approach to appropriating biblical faith—by way of wisdom.

J. Crenshaw, *Old Testament Wisdom. An Introduction* (Atlanta: John Knox Press, 1981). An introductory textbook that ranges across the entire field of wisdom concerns.

———, *Studies in Ancient Israelite Wisdom* (New York: Ktav Publishing House, 1976). A collection of valuable essays by international scholars.

R. E. Murphy, *Introduction to the Wisdom Literature of the Old Testament* (Collegeville, Minn.: Liturgical Press, 1965). An inexpensive pamphlet concerning wisdom in general.

———, *Wisdom Literature,* The Forms of the Old Testament Literature 13 (Grand Rapids: Eerdmans Publishing Co., 1981). A guide to the types of literature found in the wisdom corpus.

G. von Rad, *Wisdom in Israel* (Nashville: Abingdon, 1972). A sensitive interpretation of Israel's wisdom by a master biblical theologian.

Non-Israelite Wisdom

W. Lambert, *Babylonian Wisdom Literature* (New York: Oxford University Press, 1960). A fairly complete anthology of pertinent Mesopotamian literature.

J. B. Pritchard, *Ancient Near Eastern Texts,* rev. ed. (Princeton: Princeton University Press, ³1969). Translations of pertinent Egyptian and Mesopotamian wisdom texts.

W. K. Simpson, *The Literature of Ancient Egypt,* rev. ed. (New Haven: Yale University Press, 1973). An anthology, more complete than ANET, which also includes love poetry. See also Miriam Lichtheim, *Ancient Egyptian Literature.* 2 vols. (Berkeley: University of California Press, 1973-76).

Commentaries on Individual Books

Proverbs

W. McKane, *Proverbs, a New Approach* (Philadelphia: The Westminster Press, 1970). The best scholarly commentary, despite a questionable distinction between religious and non-religious sayings.

R. B. Y. Scott, *Proverbs, Ecclesiastes,* Anchor Bible 18 (New York: Doubleday & Co., 1965). A brief commentary, with an introduction to Wisdom Literature.

Job

F. I. Andersen, *Job* (Downers Grove, Ill.: Inter-Varsity Press, 1976). A succinct but substantial commentary, geared to any translation the reader may choose.

E. Dhorme, *A Commentary on the Book of Job* (London: Nelson, 1967). An older, but classic commentary.

R. Gordis, *The Book of God and Man: A Study of Job* (Chicago: University of Chicago Press, 1965). A solid and clear commentary.

Ecclesiastes

R. Gordis, *Koheleth, The Man and His World* (New York: Schocken Books, 1951). A sympathetic and clear exposition of the book, treating it as a whole.

Sirach

J. G. Snaith, *Ecclesiasticus,* Cambridge Bible Commentary (New York: Cambridge University Press, 1974). A brief commentary geared to the NEB translation.

Song of Songs

R. Gordis, *The Song of Songs* (New York: Jewish Theological Seminary, 1954). A solid, well-balanced explanation.

M. Pope, *Song of Songs,* Anchor Bible 7C (New York: Doubleday & Co., 1977). Very erudite study; more of an encyclopedia than a commentary.

Wisdom of Solomon

A. Wright, "Wisdom," in *The Jerome Biblical Commentary,* edited by R. Brown, J. Fitzmyer, R. E. Murphy (Englewood Cliffs, N.J.: Prentice-Hall, 1968) I, 556-68. The best short commentary available, and very perceptive.

Psalms

A. Anderson, *Book of Psalms,* New Century Bible, 2 vols. (London: Oliphants, 1972). Up-to-date and informative, with balanced judgment.

R. E. Murphy, *Psalms, Job* (Philadelphia: Fortress Press, 1978). A basic introduction to both books.

H. Ringgren, *The Faith of the Psalmists* (Philadelphia: Fortress Press, 1963). A short profile of Israel's liturgy and theology as reflected in the Psalms.

A. Weiser, *The Psalms* (Philadelphia: The Westminster Press, 1962). A scholarly commentary, but it interprets the Psalter almost exclusively in terms of the covenant renewal festival.

Studies on Israelite Theology and World of Thought

W. Eichrodt, *Theology of the Old Testament,* 2 vols. (Philadelphia: The Westminster Press, 1961-64). Israel's theology interpreted from the point of view of covenant.

S. Terrien, *The Elusive Presence* (New York: Harper & Row, 1978). A synthesis of biblical theology from the perspective of divine presence.

G. von Rad, *Old Testament Theology,* 2 vols. (New York: Harper & Row, 1962-65). A classical exposition of Israel's theology from the point of view of the transmission of traditions.

H. W. Wolff, *Anthropology of the Old Testament* (Philadelphia: Fortress Press, 1974). An excellent analysis of biblical ideas concerning the being, time, and world of humans.

The reader will find it helpful to consult biblical dictionaries, among them *The Interpreter's Dictionary of the Bible,* 4 vols. and supplementary vol. (Nashville: Abingdon, 1962-76); *Theological Dictionary of the Old Testament* (Grand Rapids: Eerdmans Publishing Co., 1974-1981), 5 vols. published thus far.

Studies in the History of Exegesis

R. M. Grant, *A Short History of the Interpretation of the Bible* (New York: Macmillan, 1963).

The Cambridge History of the Bible, 3 vols. (New York: Cambridge University Press, 1963-70).